SIGN LANGUAGE D

MW01004723

Interpretation:
A Sociolinguistic Model

Todd Tourville, CI/CT & NAD V

American Sign Language Interpreter

5501 Dickson Road
Minnetonka, MN 55345
952-939-9582 V/TTY
tttourville@stkate.edu

SIGN LANGUAGE DISSERTATION SERIES

Interpretation:
A Sociolinguistic Model

BY
DENNIS COKELY, PH.D.

LINSTOK
P R E S S

ACKNOWLEDGEMENTS

After reviewing the acknowledgement I originally wrote for this dissertation, I realize its meaning and appropriateness is even more true today that it was at the time. Thus, it appears essentially as it was. In keeping with the spirit of Linstok's Sign Language Dissertation series, and with Bill Stokoe's invaluable assistance, I have made only minor editorial modifications in the body of the text.

It is with what I hope is an appropriate blend of pride and humility that I acknowledge those to whom I am intellectually and personally indebted. I take great pride in the fact that these individuals have, for me, made possible much more than the completion of this study. I am also humbled by the fact that without them not only would this study have been impossible, but also my own understanding of the process of interpretation and human interaction would have been greatly diminished.

Much of what I have had the opportunity to write about here and elsewhere has been inspired by the many interpreters and interpreter educators whom I have had the good fortune to interact with over the years - as colleagues at meetings, seminars and conventions, or through correspondence. Each of these has in some way helped me to reflect more deeply on our collective task.

My colleagues in the Linguistics Research Lab not only helped me develop my own skills and attitudes but were totally unselfish with their time, their knowledge, and their insights about American Sign Language, Deaf people, Deaf Culture and the field of interpretation:

Bill Stokoe who, of all the people I know, still comes closest to making good on Francis Bacon's boast, "I have taken all knowledge to be my province";

Charlotte Baker-Shenk whose enthusiasm for microanalysis deepened my own appreciation for "the detail work" and whose dedication and perseverance rubbed off;

MJ Bienvenu whose openness, honesty, and trust continue to give me a better understanding of the challenges, frustrations, and joys of living with two languages and cultures.

v

There is another group that contributed much to my own thinking about the process of interpretation. Discussions with these colleagues continue to allow me to test many of my suspicions and modify some of my pre-conceived notions. In addition to the stimulating discussions that we continue to have, I value their friendship: *Betty Colonomos, Sharon Neumann Solow, Don Renzulli, Ken Rust*, and *Theresa Smith*.

Although it would be possible to single out many others who contributed to this study, the following deserve specific mention:

The interpreters who graciously and enthusiastically allowed themselves to be videotaped - I thank them for their trust; The speakers who allowed their presentations to be taped; The Board of Directors of the Conference of Interpreter Trainers who eagerly granted permission to collect the data at their 1983 conference;

MJ Bienvenu who did all of the original and verified ASL transcriptions. Shawn Davies, Sue Newburger, and Cindy Roy who did the English transcriptions;

David Knight, Charlotte Baker-Shenk, Bill Stokoe, and Micky Cokely who reviewed and commented on earlier drafts;

Deborah Tannen who was instrumental in helping me achieve a better appreciation for languaging; Roger Shuy, my mentor, whose refreshing attitudes and insights I hope I have accurately reflected;

Finally, I thank those most important to me - my family:

My parents, *Ed* and *Mary Cokely*, deserve special mention because it was they who instilled in all of their five children the value of education. I thank them for the sacrifices they made for "us kids" over the years.

My wife, *Micky*, who has taught me much and has let me teach her. She continues to be a source of constant encouragement and understanding for which I am ever-thankful. Without my best friend not only would this work have been impossible, but the joy and excitement of completion would have been lost;

Our two sons - *Scott* and *Ryan* - who not only provided welcomed diversions from this task, but who continue to help me appreciate the power, beauty, and creativity of language.

To all of these I continue to be indebted. Tennyson said "I am a part of all that I have met." I am indeed proud and humbled because I carry a part of all of these with me.

A Sociolinguistic Model of the Interpreting Process:
ASL & English

Contents

A Sociolinguistic Model of the Interpreting Process:
ASL & English

Index of Tables

Index of Figures

CHAPTER ONE

INTERPRETATION: AN OVERVIEW

Translation is often used as a generic term to refer to the transfer of thoughts and ideas from one language (source or sL[1]) to another language (target or tL) regardless of the form of either language (written, spoken, or signed). When the form of the source Language (sL) is either spoken or signed and the form of the target Language (tL) is either spoken or signed, the transfer process is referred to as interpretation (Brislin, 1976). The magnitude of this task is such that it has been called "...probably the most complex type of event yet produced in the evolution of the cosmos" (Richards, 1953: 250). While this may overstate the case, interpretation is undeniably a complex cognitive process.

The need for, and the services of, interpreters has its earliest documentation in the legendary or mythical accounts (e.g. The Tower of Babel), as well as strictly historical accounts (e.g. the conquests of Alexander the Great) of antiquity. Indeed, it has probably always been the case that, to some extent, members of a linguistic minority community have relied upon interpreters to facilitate social, political, and economic interaction with members of a linguistic majority community. This is perhaps most apparent when one examines the linguistic and communicative interaction between Deaf and hearing communities.

Sign Language interpreters, with varying degrees of competence, have probably always been a vital factor in the lives of members of the Deaf Community. Historically, hearing persons with Deaf family members, teachers of Deaf students and religious workers have functioned in the interpreting role. However, in the U.S. federal legislation (P.L. 94-142 and P.L. 95-539) and the accessibility demands of the Deaf Community have resulted in an increased demand for Sign Language interpreters in legal, educational, medical, occupational, religious, and social situations. In response to this demand, an increasing number of Interpreter Preparation Programs have been established in colleges and universities. In 1982, for example, there were a total of 80 such programs.

Needed: a model of the interpretation process

Despite the growing acceptance of and demand for Sign Language Interpreters and despite the dramatic rise of the number of Interpreter Preparation Programs, very little is known about the process of interpreting. The need for research in this area was underscored by a conference on Interpreter Research sponsored by the National Academy of Gallaudet College (Per-Lee, 1981). At that conference it was made clear that an understanding of the interpreting process was necessary in order to address some of the major concerns facing preparation programs and consumers (e.g. evaluation/certification, entrance and exit criteria, curriculum and materials development).

While various models of the interpreting process have been proposed (Ingram, 1974, Gerver, 1976, Moser, 1978, Ford, 1981), their heuristic utility is limited by the fact that they adopt an information processing perspective in which the interpreter is viewed primarily as a mediator between two languages. However, it can be argued that the interpreter mediates between two individuals and communities as well as mediating between two languages. In this respect, the study of interpretation is a sociolinguistic problem and must be studied along the parameters that determine sociolinguistic entities, "...whether from the point of view of languages or ... of the processes at play in the adaptation of a message to a receiver with a different linguistic and cultural background" (Pergnier, 1978). Thus, for the full descriptive/explanatory power of any model to be realized, it must be set within the context of those sociolinguistic factors that obtain in any communicative situation.

The specific problems addressed in this study can be stated as follows: what sociolinguistic factors influence the interpretation process; can a sociolinguistically sensitive model of the interpretation process be developed, and what are the applications and implications of such a model?

Even a cursory examination of preparation programs for Sign Language interpreters highlights the need for a clearer understanding of the process of interpretation. Unlike preparation programs in spoken language interpretation that are almost exclusively graduate level programs (e.g. the Monterey Institute for International Studies and the Geneva University School of Translation and Interpretation), until recently, there were no graduate level preparation programs for Sign Language interpretation (see, e.g., (Witter-Merithew, 1980). In fact, in 1980, 66% of the programs were two-year programs (A.A. or A.S.), 7% were four-year programs (B.A. or B.S.), and 27% were short term, non-degree programs (ranging from ten weeks to one year). Since these degree programs are all at the undergraduate level, they often lack the flexibility and autonomy associated with graduate level programs. This can be clearly seen, for example, by examining the entry requirements for these degree programs. The majority of them (66%) have no stated entry requirements in either ASL or English; of those that do, only 10% have an English entry requirement and only 6% have an ASL entry requirement (however, 30% of the programs do have a general "basic or intermediate sign language" entry requirement).

Another indication of the need for a clearer understanding of the interpreting process is the content and scope of the curricula used in Interpreter Preparation Programs. Course descriptions from 25 degree programs indicate that all of the programs include courses required by their respective colleges (e.g. General Psychology, English Composition, Physical Education). All of the programs have language development courses (e.g. Beginning Sign Language, Manual Communication IV, Introduction to ASL) which are required in the first two semesters and often are required in the third and fourth semesters. Courses that specifically focus on interpreting typically do not appear until the second or third semester. It is not unusual for the total number of interpretation-specific courses to comprise less than one-third of the total number of required courses. It is clear that the variability in Interpreter Preparation Programs exists, in part, because of the lack of empirically-based descriptions of the interpreting process upon which to base curricula.

The lack of descriptive studies of the interpreting process has also negatively affected the certification procedures used by the Registry of Interpreters for the Deaf (RID). It has been suggested (Coulton, 1982) that the pre-1988 RID evaluations were neither reliable nor valid. The lack of reliability may have been due to the fact that the evaluators lacked a clear understanding of what it was they were evaluating (i.e. the interpreting process). The lack of validity may have been due, in part, to the fact that candidates were asked to interpret texts which, historically, did not reflect realistic interpreting situations or natural language use (NESSC Committee, 1983). Finally, the composition of evaluation teams prior to 1983 (three deaf evaluators and two hearing evaluators) may have produced results that were more indicative of candidates' conversational signing ability than of their interpreting ability since the majority of evaluators (i.e. the deaf evaluators) lacked access to one of the languages involved and were thus unable to compare interpreted message with original messages (Cokely, 1982).

In short, the need for a clearer understanding of the interpreting process has been and continues to be evident at all levels of preparation and evaluation. A verified model of the interpreting process has direct application for determining entrance and exit criteria for preparation programs, for designing curricula and instructional materials, and for designing assessment procedures and materials. Additionally, such a model would provide the basis for future systematic research in the area.

Research on interpretation

Although it is safe to say that the interpretation of (spoken or signed) languages predates the translation of (written) texts, it is nevertheless the case that translation has received the bulk of theoretical and descriptive attention (see e.g. (Steiner, 1975) (Amos, 1920). Undoubtedly one of the reasons for this lack of interest in interpreting is that it was not until 1946 with the War Crime Trials in Nuremberg that the importance of interpreting as a profession was recognized. Since that time, however, there has been "...disappointingly little actual research carried out by either psychologists, linguists, or teachers of interpretation." (Gerver, 1976).

The first thorough discussion and analysis of (spoken-to-spoken) interpreting was undertaken by a conference interpreter (Paneth, 1957). Although the focus of Paneth's work was on the preparation of interpreters, her observations of interpreters at actual conferences led her to note that interpreters often lag from 2 to 4 seconds behind the source Language (sL) message. In addition, Paneth discussed certain problems faced by interpreters (e.g. how the sL message is segmented, and the use the interpreter makes of speaker pauses). The earliest experimental studies appeared in 1965 (Treisman, 1965, Oléron & Nanpon 1965). Treisman's study was not directly concerned with interpretation, but rather with the effects of sequential constraints of messages on two speech transmission tasks. The tasks were shadowing and interpretation. Although some of the subjects were bilinguals, none was an experienced interpreter. Not surprising, the results showed a greater "lag" (or ear-voice span) for interpreting than for shadowing. Oléron and Nanpon confirmed this by showing that the interpreter's lag time could range from 2 to 10 seconds with the length of the lag time being determined by the relative difficulty of the incoming message.

Gerver (Gerver, 1969) investigated the effects of the rate of transmission of the incoming message on interpreter accuracy. Using pre-recorded passages at increasing rates (95, 112, 120, 142, and 164 words per minute), he was able to demonstrate that the proportion of information correctly interpreted decreased with each increase in rate. This study confirmed an earlier suggestion (Seleskovitch, 1975) that the optimal rate of input for interpreters is between 95 and 120 words per minute.

Barik (Barik, 1969) suggested that interpreters use pauses in the incoming message as one means of delineating units of meaning. (Goldman-Eisler, 1972) demonstrated that interpreters employ one of three strategies in their use of pauses: encoding the "chunks" between pauses (identity); starting to encode a "chunk" before it has been fully delivered by the speaker (fission); and stringing together two or more "chunks" (fusion). (Gerver, 1971), by comparing the interpretation of input texts that did and did not contain speaker pauses, concluded that sL pauses do assist the interpreter in segmenting, understanding, and encoding messages. Barik (Barik, 1973) undertook a computer analysis of the temporal characteristics of recordings of speaker's and interpreter's speech. He concluded that interpreters do make use of speaker pauses and, interestingly, are engaged in speaking for a greater proportion of the time than the speaker.

Experimental research has also shown that, despite having to listen and speak simultaneously, interpreters are able to carry out complex cognitive tasks. Gerver (Gerver, 1974) demonstrated that comprehension of input messages was higher after interpreting than after simple repetition of input messages, but not as high as with active listening. Thus, the task of interpreting does not preclude or hinder the performance of concurrent cognitive tasks. However, the task of interpreting may place some limits on the efficiency of performance (Gerver, 1976).

There have been only two attempts to analyze the content and quality of interpreted messages. The first (Gerver, 1969) specified eight categories that account for differences between the original and interpreted messages: omissions of words, omissions of phrases, omissions of longer input stretches (eight words or more), substitution of words, substitution of phrases, correction of words, and correction of phrases. The second (Barik, 1973) proposed three major categories omissions, additions, and substitutions, with several sub-categories of each (e.g. skipping omissions, comprehension omissions, delay omissions, and compounding omissions). The Gerver study and the Barik study were experimental in nature, using pre-recorded audio-tapes as the sL input. As noted in Gerver (1976), both Gerver's and Barik's methods of classifying errors and omissions can be questioned due to the subjective criteria initially used to determine errors and the fact that the overt unit of analysis in both studies seems to be "words" rather than meaning. That is, if a word were omitted, added, or substituted, then an error was presumed to occur, regardless of whether the meaning conveyed by that word was conveyed successfully by the interpreter by other means (i.e. other than the use of a separate lexical item). Another limitation of the Gerver and Barik studies is that they sample the performance of interpreters in a clinical/experimental rather than a realistic setting (i.e. with a live speaker and audience).

Despite the paucity of research on interpreting and the clinical nature of such research, there have been two attempts to account for research findings in the formulation of models of the interpreting process. Both models (Gerver, 1976, Moser, 1978) are basically flow charts drawing heavily on theory and research in human information processing. Gerver's model of the interpreting process is "...essentially a psychological rather than a linguistic description..." (Gerver, 1976: 196). Moser's model, though more complex, is an elaboration of an information processing model (Massaro, 1975a, 1975b) that tries to "...describe the activities involved in understanding and producing language" (Moser 1978: 353). The focus of both models is the interpreter's organization and access of syntactic and semantic information. Thus, the interpreter is viewed primarily as a mediator between two languages. However, it can be argued that the interpreter mediates between two individuals and communities as well as mediating between two languages. In this respect, the study of interpretation is a sociolinguistic problem and must be studied along the parameters that determine sociolinguistic entities, "...whether from the point of view of languages or...of the processes at play in the adaptation of a message to a receiver with a different linguistic and cultural background." (Pergnier 1978: 203). Thus, for the full explanatory/descriptive power of any model to be realized, it must be set within the context of those sociolinguistic factors that obtain in any communicative situation.

Research on sign language Interpretation

In addition to the studies of interpretation discussed above (all of which involved spoken languages as both source and target Language), there have been a few studies of interpretation in which one of the languages (generally the Target Language) was a signed language. Two studies sought to develop a psychological/personality profile of Sign Language interpreters (Quigley, et al, 1973, Schein, 1974). Quigley and his associates report that their subjects (N=30) possessed the following characteristics or traits: above average intelligence measured by the Wechsler Adult Intelligence Scale, above average in creative thinking ability on the Christensen-Guilford Fluency Test, well above average for those under the age of 45 in their ability to organize materials in space on the Minnesota Paper Form Board Test, and at or above the mean on all personality factors (except one - the need to make a good impression) on the California Psychological Inventory. Schein focused on the personality of a group of interpreters (N=17) using the Edwards Personality Preference Schedule. He reports that the interpreters in his study fit the description of someone who is "...desirous of being the center of attention, wants to be independent, is not expecting help from others, is not afraid to make errors, and is not perseverative." (Schein 1974: 39).

Neither study was able to correlate findings with subjects' interpretation competence. Funding for the Quigley, et.al. study terminated before analysis of the subjects' interpreting performance could be undertaken. Schein used a panel of 6 judges to rate the interpreting performance of his subjects on a five-point scale. However, the ratings of the judges did not correlate highly and, in fact, "...seem to contain a large component of error." (Schein 1974: 42). Thus, while both studies shed some light on the psychological/personality characteristics or traits of individuals attracted to or working in the field of Sign Language interpreting, they fail to identify those characteristics or traits, if any, that might separate competent from less than competent interpreters. A number of educational studies over the past two decades have investigated the extent to which Deaf high school or college students comprehend information under different communication conditions, including interpretation. However, since the focus of these studies (e.g. (Newell, 1978, Jacobs, 1977, Caccamise and Blasdell, 1977) was on student comprehension and not interpretation per se, no information on interpreter performance in these studies is available. Additionally, in at least some of these studies (e.g. Jacobs 1977; Caccamise and Blasdell 1977) the "interpreted" stimulus material was memorized or rehearsed and, as such, does not represent either actual interpretation nor interpreter behavior.

Only a few studies have addressed the question of the performance of Sign Language interpreters. Brasel (Brasel, 1976), underscoring the mental and physical demands of the interpreting task, demonstrated that after twenty minutes an interpreter's accuracy decreases significantly, presumably due to mental and physical fatigue. Hurwitz (Hurwitz, 1980) has shown, as one might expect, that experienced interpreters are more accurate than inexperienced interpreters in interpreting situations where the sL is ASL and the tL is English. Llewellyn-Jones (Llewellyn-Jones, 1981), in a study of British Sign Language (BSL) interpreters, investigated the time lag between a spoken English message and the BSL interpretation of that message and concluded that there was a "...very low average lag shown by even the most effective interpreters." (Llewellyn-Jones 1981:96). Cokely (Cokely, 1982), examining interpreter performance in the medical interview setting, offered the following classification of interpreter miscues or errors: perception, memory, semantic, performance. Finally, Cokely (Cokely, 1983) examined the extent to which interpreters convey speaker affect and determined that there are significant differences and limits in the extent to which speaker affect is conveyed by Sign Language interpreters.

As in the case of spoken language interpretation, the lack of research has not deterred individuals from proposing models of the interpreting process. As with models proposed for spoken language interpretation, these models are essentially based on information processing theory. Ingram (Ingram, 1974) views the interpreter as a channel through which deaf and hearing people communicate. Ford (Ford, 1981) views the interpreter as a facilitator of communication or a communication specialist, and adopts an information processing approach in which the task is to receive, decode, encode, and transmit messages.

The lack of research in the area of interpretation, and more specifically Sign Language interpretation, and the focus of that research merely underscores the need for and ultimate value of a more socio-linguistically sensitive view of the interpreting process. Since the field of translation has received more theoretical and descriptive attention than the field of interpretation, and since, at some basic level, the two fields may represent different realizations of the same process, it will be helpful to review the literature pertaining to translation.

Translation process studies

Although the interpretation of (spoken or signed) languages predates the translation of (written) texts, translation has received the bulk of theoretical and descriptive attention.

Undoubtedly, this is in large measure due to the "permanent presence" of both the source and target messages in translation (Kopczynski, 1980) compared with the "transient presence" of source and target messages in interpretation. This "permanent presence" has encouraged a dual focus in the field of translation studies: a study of the translation process (the factors involved and the underlying strategies) and a study of the translation product (the qualitative comparison of source text and translated text) (Wilss, 1982).

The study of the translation process has yielded no less than sixteen types of models that attempt to describe the translation process. As Bathgate (Bathgate, 1981) has pointed out, "These models differ because they refer to different aspects or phases of the translation process..." The hermeneutic model (Steiner, 1975) focuses on the translation of biblical texts but applies, *mutatis mutandis*, to the translation of any text. The situational model (Richards, 1953, Catford, 1965) focuses on the fact that the meaning of a text is conditioned by the situation in which it was made or in which it is understood to be made. The stylistic model (Wilss, 1977) focuses on the fact that the translator is often faced with the choice of attending to the form of the text or to the content of the text. The word-by-word model (Catford 1965) focuses on the replacement of a sL unit (the word or phrase level but rarely at the sentence level) with a tL unit as is often done in language teaching. The syntactic model (Yngve, 1957, Tosh, 1965), developed primarily for machine translation, focuses on the relationship between words in sentences. The transformational model (Nida, 1964, 1974) focuses on the analysis of the sL text by reduction to "kernel sentences" and the transfer of the "kernel sentences" to the tL. The interlingua model (Droste, 1969) focuses on the fact that the translator's understanding of a text is expressed mentally by a language that is neither sL nor tL. The semantic model (Ogden, 1927), which was developed with reference to the meaning of language as such, focuses on the arbitrary relationship between referent, symbol, and thought. The information theory model (Richards 1953; Nida 1964) focuses on the notion of message redundancy and draws heavily on models developed for telecommunications. The nomenclative model (Bathgate 1981) focuses on how a translator handles untranslatable terms, e.g. technical terms. The modulation model (Vinay and Darbelnet, 1958) is related to the situational model in that it focuses on the fact that there is a need to say things in different ways in different cultures. The generative model (Levy, 1967) is based on games theory and focuses on the fact that the translation process involves a large number of decisions that affect later stages of a translation. The integral model (Holmes, 1978) focuses on the need for the translator to adopt an overall translation strategy in order to ensure textual consistency in the translation. The normative model (Van den Broek, and Lefevere, 1979) focuses on the translation use of certain "translation standards" to judge the linguistic and factual accuracy of a translation. The three-stage checking model (Bathgate 1981) addresses the decisions a translator faces when determining whether to translate literally, according to the meaning of the text, or according to the situational constraints of the text. The interactive model (Bathgate 1981) focuses on the fact that the sL text must be interactive with and reconciled to the background knowledge that the translator brings to the translation task.

While each of these models may be sufficient for the limited set of factors each attempts to account for and for that portion of the translation process that each chooses to highlight, as House (House, 1981) notes, "...they have hitherto not proved to be of immediate usefulness in solving the practical problems of describing and assessing translations as finished products." This recognition of the practical limitations and applications of theoretical process models has, in part, resulted in theoretical and descriptive work that focuses on the results of the translation process - the translated text.

Translation product studies

Observations on the nature of the translated text and translation quality date from Cicero: *ut orator—ut interpres*, 'a translation should be free—a translation should be literal'. These vague and apparently contradictory requirements for assessing translation quality have been restated in the literature in various ways. (Savory, 1968: 50) summarizes the various "principles" that have been used to assess translation quality:

1. A translation must give the words of the original.
2. A translation must give the ideas of the original.
3. A translation should read like an original work.
4. A translation should read like a translation.
5. A translation should reflect the style of the original.
6. A translation should possess the style of the translator.
7. A translation should read as a contemporary of the original.
8. A translation should read as a contemporary of the translator.
9. In a translation, a translator must never add or leave out anything.
10. In a translation, a translator may, if need be, add or leave out something.

More recent, communicatively oriented studies have resulted in an array of criteria that can be used to assess the quality of a translated work. For example, a "good" translation is one that accomplishes the same purpose in the tL as the original accomplished in the sL (Forster, 1958) or arouses the same effect as the original (Zilahy, 1963). Nida (1964) has proposed that translations be judged according to three criteria: 1) general efficiency of the communication process; 2) comprehension of intent; 3) equivalence of response. (Similar criteria have been offered by Nida and Taber (1975) This third criterion, equivalence of response, is related to Nida's well-known principle of "Dynamic Equivalence of a Translation" (1964: 159).

Other authors have also addressed the notion of equivalence in translation. However, the discussions of this notion of translation equivalence (TE) most often result in the advancement of a new label for the requirement of TE with no attempt to determine how the "TE concept" can be tested. A review of recent TE terminology yields the following: "Total equivalence" (Albrecht, 1973), "functional equivalence" (Jager, 1973), "equivalence in difference" (Jakobson 1966), "illusionist vs. anti-illusionist translation" (Levy 1967), "closest natural equivalent" (Nida 1964), "formal correspondence vs. dynamic equivalence" (Nida 1964), "stylistic equivalence" (Popovic, 1977), "pragmatic appropriateness" (Kopczynski 1980), and "text pragmatic equivalence" (Wilss 1982).

While it is intuitively desirable that a translation should be "equivalent" to the original, such a requirement is of limited value if it cannot be empirically tested (House 1981). Several methods have been suggested by which TE can be empirically assessed. Nida and Taber (1974) suggest the following:

1. The Cloze technique in which textual comprehensibility is equated with text predictability;
2. Eliciting reactions to several translation alternatives;
3. A referential explanation task;
4. Reading a translation aloud before an audience.

Other approaches to assessing TE have been offered by Miller and Beebe-Center (1958):

1. Use of a panel of judges;
2. Comparison with a translation of "granted excellence;"
3. Use of a comprehension test with a group of respondents.

Apart from the inherent limitations of each of these suggested procedures (for discussion, see House 1981: 10-21), they seem more suited to experimental investigations of translation quality than to guiding and assisting the translation practitioner. Consequently, a number of translation "rules" and "practical principles" have been offered to guide the practitioner. In general, these "rules" take the form of presenting alternatives for dealing with specific translation problems. Although others have proposed translation "rules" or "principles" (e.g. Whitehouse 1973; Landsberg 1976), the most comprehensive presentation can be found in the work of Newmark (1969; 1973; 1974a; 1974b; 1981).

Newmark's basic approach is that problems of translation are closely related to problems of linguistic analysis. Thus, he addresses translation problems in terms of recurring linguistic (and cross-linguistic) issues that the translator faces. For example, Newmark's (1973) "Twenty-Three Restricted Rules of Translation" includes discussion of sL collocations, semantic ranges, titles, and quotations. His "Further Propositions on Translation I" (1974a) and "Further Propositions on Translation II" (1974b) discuss evaluative language, register, text cohesion, referential synonymy, paraphrase, jargon, ideolect, and other topics. His *Approaches to Translation* (1981) offers 145 propositions or principles, dealing with issues such as semantic categories, idioms, metaphor, context, variation, back-translation, cultural allusions, and punctuation.

Despite offering "rules" or "principles" for the translator, Newmark admits that translation will never be an exact science. He further states that "...the concept of the 'ideal translation' is unreal. Translation is an 'endless' procedure...translations can never be finished, only laid aside. They can always be improved." (Newmark 1981: 148).

The relationship between interpretation & translation

While it would seem that the theoretical and descriptive work in the area of translation would be applicable to the area of interpretation, there are significant differences between the two fields that limit the usefulness of this work. It is true, however, that the essential goal of taking a message originally expressed in one language (sL) and conveying that message in another language (tL) is similar for the translator and the interpreter. The essence of translation and interpretation, then, is the preservation of meaning across two languages, cultures, and communities. (This is one reason why the term 'translation' is used as a generic term to refer to both translation and interpretation.) Perhaps the most important difference between translation and interpretation is the nature of the texts with which translators and interpreters work. The translator's text is written and, therefore, "...permanently at the translator's disposal..." (Wilss 1982: 56) while the interpreter's text is spoken or signed and "...presented but once; it is, so to say, 'transient'..." (Kopczynski 1980: 24). Thus, the translator is relatively free from the constraints and pressures imposed by time. That is, the interpreter is constrained by having momentary access to the sL message, while the translator generally is under no such constraint. This textual difference has several important implications for how translators work, because:

1. The text is permanently at the translator's disposal; thus, the translator is able to review the text in its entirety before beginning to translate;
2. The text and its translation are written; the translator can refer back to previously translated sections and passages;
3. The translation can be reviewed; the translator has the option of seeking feedback from both bilingual and monolingual reviewers;
4. The translated text can be reviewed; the translator can make corrections.

The second significant difference between translation and interpretation is the nature of the relationship between the translator and the original text author and the translated text recipient(s). Often the translator does not know the author of the original text (Wilss 1982), while the interpreter must know as much about the speaker as possible (Namy 1978). Thus, the translator may lack sufficient knowledge of the author's background and personality to determine accurately and faithfully the author's intended meaning (Landsberg 1976; Wilss 1982). On the other hand, the translator often does not know the readers or recipients of the translated text while, with the exception of radio and television broadcasts, the interpreter always works in the presence of recipients or addresses. The limited feedback available to the translator may result in a failure to account sufficiently for the effects of sociocultural distance on the recipient's understanding of the translated text (Taber 1980).

Given the differences in the nature of sL texts and the nature of the relationships with text originator and text recipient, it is only at the most basic level of interlingual mediation of messages that translation and interpretation can be viewed as the same process. Thus, the theoretical and descriptive work in the field of translation must only be selectively and carefully applied to the field of interpretation.

Summary, Chapter 1

The ultimate aim of interpretation is, in part, the re-expression in one language of a message originally delivered in another language in such a way that the interpretation is "...clear, unambiguous, and immediately comprehensible, that is to say perfectly idiomatic, so that the listener does not have to mentally re-interpret what reaches him..." (Namy 1978: 26). In order to accomplish this aim, it is apparent that the interpreter not only must mediate between two languages but, perhaps more basically, must mediate between individuals, communities, and cultures (Pergnier 1978). Successful mediation between individuals, languages, and cultures is only possible if the interpreter is consciously or unconsciously aware of what ethnographic studies have shown. To be more specific, the interpreter must be aware of the fact that "...communities differ significantly in ways of speaking, in patterns of repertoire and switching, in the roles and meaning of speech. They (ethnographies) indicate differences with regard to beliefs, values, reference groups, norms, and the like." (Hymes 1972: 42).

A sociolinguistically sensitive model of the process of interpretation from spoken American English to American Sign Language is presented in the following chapters.

Note

[1] The generally accepted convention in the literature on interpretation is to use SL when refering to the Source Language. The same pair of capital letters, however, is used in the literature on Sign Language research and linguistics used when refering to Sign Language. Therefore, in order to avoid confusion, *sL* will be used to refer to source Language and, in order to maintain consistency, *tL* will be used to refer to Target Language. This use of lower case s or t and upper case L also offers the serendipitous advantage of constantly drawing one's attention to the fact that the process of interpretation is only possible when one is working with Languages.

CHAPTER TWO

INTERPRETATION AS MEDIATION

The interpreter is engaged in a constant process in which a range of components influencing the participants and the SL message must be assessed and in which the effect of any influencing component must be accurately and appropriately accounted for in the tL message. In examining the components that affect any communicative behavior (and, thus, those components that the interpreter must be aware of), it is possible to identify components that pertain to the context within which the interaction occurs and components that pertain to the nature of the communicative message itself. Thus, a sociolinguistically sensitive and accurate model can be constructed.

Interaction Factors

Brown and Fraser (1979) have proposed a taxonomy that identifies the components of the situation (i.e. context) within which interaction occurs. The major components of their taxonomy are: setting, purpose, and participants.

A. *Setting* accounts for a range of environmental factors that may affect communicative interaction. The locale of the interaction may influence the linguistic and non-linguistic activities of participants. This is especially true in settings that hold cultural expectations or taboos (Hymes, 1972). The locale of the interaction may also influence the physical orientation of the participants toward each other (e.g. a lecture or a formal dinner) which, in turn, may affect the linguistic and communicative interaction of participants (Moscovici & Plon, 1966; Fielding & Coope, 1976).

Apart from the interaction locale, communicative interaction may be influenced by the temporal setting in which it occurs. Thus, greeting and leavetaking formulae depend upon the time of day; lexical selection and use in some languages is determined by the time of day (Fillmore, 1975) and, in general, deictic forms are only completely intelligible if one is aware of the physical and temporal setting in which they are used.

A third aspect of the setting addresses the presence or absence of bystanders in the environment who, although not taking part in the interaction, may influence the communicative behavior of the participants. This may take the form of requiring participants to use restricted registers or codes in the presence of certain bystanders (Dixon, 1982), or may be motivated by a desire for secrecy and, for example, take the form of spelling out parts of a message when in the presence of children (*"Let's buy some c-a-n-d-y for later"*). In any event, it is clear that the presence or absence of bystanders can influence the participants' interaction, if only to the extent that the participants must be aware of certain bystander honorifics (Comrie, 1976).

B. *Purpose:* this component accounts for those factors that direct the participants' activities throughout a situation until the communicative event is completed (Brown and Fraser, 1979). The purpose of any communicative event is influenced by the type of activity called for in the event and the subject matter of topic of communication (Chafe, 1972; Keenan and Schieffelin, 1976). Certain types of activities (e.g. buying, selling, lecturing, playing a game) place constraints on the goals, participant roles, discourse structure, and, to some extent, the participants and the setting. More importantly, activity types constrain or define the participant's purposes. The significance of activity type can be seen, for example, in the effect on the nature of turn-taking (Schegloff, 1972), conversational inferencing (Gumperz, 1977), and conversational strategies available to participants (Blom and Gumperz, 1972).

Apart from the activity type, the subject matter also influences the participant's purpose. As Brown and Fraser point out, "...an activity type specifies the range of possible purposes that participants will orient toward in the activity, but not which specific one will be involved." (1979: 43). While it is clearly not possible to specify the enormous range of subject matter that people discuss, the influence of subject matter on interaction has been shown in a number of studies. Labov (1972) has shown that emotionally charged subject matter can lead to stylistic changes, Linde and Labov (1975) and Linde (1981) have shown that different subject matter influences discourse structure and syntactic structure, and, of course, it is obvious that subject matter influences choice of lexicon.

C. *Participants:* this component accounts for factors specific to individual participants or to the relationship(s) between participants. As for individual participants, there are factors that pertain to the individual as an individual and those that pertain to the individual as a member of a particular social group.

The individualistic factors can be either temporary states and attitudes or relatively stable aspects that influence a person's communicative interaction. A temporary state of anxiety or fear, for example, will influence an individual's linguistic behavior (Labov, 1972) as will a temporary state of joy or anger (Pronovost, 1942). Indeed, Ostwald (1963) concludes that emotional states influence a person's vocal communication despite efforts to repress them. Temporary physical states (e.g. a cold) will likewise affect linguistic behavior. The influence of the relatively stable states of individual and social identity have been amply documented. Phonological, syntactic, semantic, and/or paralinguistic aspects of communicative behavior will be affected, for example, by a person's age (e.g. Helfrich, 1979; Laver and

Trudgill, 1979), gender (e.g. Smith, 1979; Lakoff, 1975), personality (e.g. Scherer, 1979; Ramsay, 1966), social identity (e.g. Labov, 1966; Shuy, 1969; Wolfram and Fasold, 1974), and ethnicity (e.g. Shuy, Baratz, and Wolfram, 1969; Shuy, 1977; Wolfram and Fasold, 1974).

The actual or perceived relationship between participants will also influence their communicative interaction. This is most clearly seen when participants take on certain roles or interact with each other on the basis of certain role expectations. In such situations communicative interaction is often characterized by the use of particular registers. Studies of occupational roles have provided the most information about registers. Thus, there is evidence to suggest that the use of distinctive registers can be found in the communicative behavior of doctors (Robinson, 1980; Shuy, 1977), school teachers (Sinclair and Coulthard, 1975), radio commentators (Crystal and Davy, 1969), and stockbrokers (Turner, 1973). Other role-related registers include Baby Talk (Snow, 1972), Foreigner Talk (Ferguson, 1971; Ferguson and DeBose, 1977), as well as the distinctive speech of professional gamblers (Maurer, 1950), smugglers (Bradley, 1956), drug addicts (Agar, 1973), and members of the underworld (Halliday, 1976).

The best described characteristic of these registers is the lexicon which may involve the use of technical terms, commonly used lexical items that have "in-group" meanings, or novel lexical items. However, registers are not merely characterized by their lexicon. They may, for example, involve novel and complex extensions of the semantic range of common words. Thus, as Turner (1973) points out, stockholders attribute animate qualities to inanimate goods and commodities (e.g. *tin soars, oil suffers*). In addition, distinctive syntactic structures and phonological features can characterize certain registers. For example, the complex syntactic structures and nominal pronunciation of the university lecturer (Brown and Fraser, 1979) is quite different from the way caretakers or mothers talk to young children

(Snow and Ferguson, 1977). Finally, at least in the case of teacher talk, there is evidence that discourse strategies may also characterize certain registers (Sinclair and Coutlhard, 1975). For example, it is perhaps unique to educational settings that in question-answer sequences the questioner (i.e. teacher) generally knows the answers in advance.

Message Factors

Setting, purpose, and participants are contextual factors or components that influence any communicative interaction. These in slightly changed order are the first three elements of the well-known SPEAKING mnemonic of Hymes (1972). These three (S-setting and scene, P-participants; E-ends as purpose, goals and ends) appear to have a different focus from that of the remaining five elements of the mnemonic. That is, these three clearly deal with the situation, while the remaining elements deal with the nature of the communicative message. Although it is true that the nature of any communicative message may be influenced (and perhaps determined) by the setting, purpose, and participants; nevertheless, since the interpreter's task centers to a large extent on the message, it is necessary to examine those factors that affect the nature of messages and to accord them a status distinct from that of the situational factors.

D. *Message Form and Message Content* (Hymes' A-"act sequence"): these two factors account for the fact that "...how something is said is part of what is said" (Hymes, 1972: 59). Thus, the form of the message must be attended to, since message form can condition and even control content. The content of a message is crucial inasmuch as topic (or topic change, maintenance, and elaboration) is indicated by message content. The ability of participants to know what is being discussed, when the topic of discussion has changed, and when and how to maintain the topic is not only crucial for discourse analysis but is also a clear indication that the communicative competence of individuals includes the ability to distinguish message form and content.

E. *Message Key* (Hymes' K-"key") : this factor accounts for the tone, manner, or spirit with which a message is conveyed (e.g. humorous or serious). Message key can often be signaled by nonverbal means (e.g. wink, gesture, style of dress) or stylistic means (e.g. vowel lengthening for emphasis). However, stylistic means of signaling message key may not always reflect the mood or tone of the speaker (as in the use of certain politeness formulae). The significance of message key is obvious when one realizes that it can contradict or even supersede the surface content of a message.

F. *Message Channel and Language Form* (Hymes' I-"instrumentalities") : these two factors account for the channel of transmission of a message and the inherent variability of languages. Messages may be spoken, signed, written or conveyed via some other channel of transmission (e.g. semaphore). Within each transmission channel it is also possible to identify certain message modes (e.g. singing or whistling). The importance of message channel is apparent when one considers the respective capacities and limitations of each channel may preclude certain message modes (e.g. whistling in sign). The language form factor addresses the issues of message intelligibility. The inherent variability of languages (realized as geographic, social, or other dialectal variation) suggests that the intelligibility of any message depends, in part, on the extent to which participants use mutually intelligible language forms in expressing messages. Since some language forms derive from others "...by addition, deletion, substitution and permutation in various combinations" (Hymes, 1972: 63), it is obvious that in order to understand a message accurately it must be expressed in a form that is intelligible to the intended addressee. (Note: it is this very point, extended interlingually rather than intralingually, that is the *raison d'etre* for interpretation.)

G. *Interaction Norms and Interpretation Norms* (Hymes' N-"norms") : these two factors account for specific behaviors that precede, accompany, or follow communicative interaction and the fact that both speaker and addressee must attribute the same meaning and significance to those behaviors. Thus, for example, speaker and addressee must share the same turn-taking behaviors and/or understand the intent of such behaviors. An awareness of and understanding of these norms presupposes understanding of the social structure and social relationships within a given community as well as the values and beliefs of the community.

H. *Discourse Genre* (Hymes' G-"genre") : this factor accounts for the fact that different types of discourse can be distinguished on the basis of certain formal characteristics. Thus, on the basis of an analysis of message form it is possible to establish certain discourse categories or genres (e.g. narratives, lectures, prayers, proverbs). Although it is generally true that certain genres often coincide with specific settings (e.g. prayers in a church), they may occur in a range of settings and thus must be treated independent of setting. In addition, since any given discourse genre will influence the previous four factors, it is crucial to treat this factor in an analytically independent fashion. Figure 2.1 on the following page is adapted from Brown and Fraser (1979). It summarizes the factors that influence the communicative behavior of individuals and thus influence the interpreter's task. As was noted above, these factors are separated into two major divisions--factors that pertain to the context and factors that pertain to the message itself.

Figure 2.1 shows factors that influence any communicative interaction, including those interactions mediated by an interpreter, but the present categorization of message-specific factors lacks equivalent analytical specificity: different discourse genres

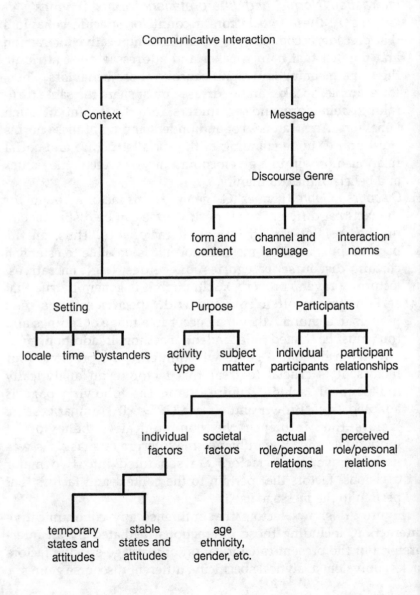

Figure 2.1. Factors Influencing communicative interaction.

Expository monologues

The data analyzed in this study are all of the same discourse genre; i.e. the lecture. Thus, it is necessary to further specify factors that influence that discourse genre. In order to do this, the literature on discourse analysis as it pertains to lectures must be examined. The term discourse analysis has been used to refer both to the analysis of dialogue and the analysis of monologue (Longacre, 1983). Descriptive studies in the field of discourse analysis have revealed much about certain types of discourse and less about other types. For example, much attention has been given to narratives (e.g. Tannen, 1979; Chafe, 1980; Prince, 1982), jokes (e.g. Sacks, 1974; Linde, 1981), myths and fairy tales (e.g. Propp, 1968; McLendon, 1982). However, there is relatively little descriptive information on the type of discourse that is of interest in this study - lectures. General observations have been made, however, about some of the characteristics of lectures.

Classroom lectures and perhaps, by extension, all types of lectures, are nonreciprocal (Lakoff, 1982). That is, unlike nominal conversations, participants do not share control of the discourse. Thus, in a lecture, "...one participant...does most of the speaking and determines the start and finish of the discourse." (Lakoff, 1982: 27). In addition, the selection of topic(s) is generally determined by the lecturer. In short, the lecture is more properly thought of as an expository monologue.

Longacre (1983) offers a set of parameters for classifying discourse types that, when applied to expository monologues, reveals further characteristics of this discourse type. He posits four binary parameters: chronological linkage, agent reference, projection, and tension. Chronological linkage refers to "...a framework of temporal succession in which some (often most) of the events or doings are contingent on previous events or doings" (Longacre, 1983: 3). Agent reference refers to "...orientation towards agents with at least a partial identity of agent reference running through the discourse" (ibid.:3). Projection refers to "...a situation or action which is contemplated, enjoined, or anticipated but not realized" (ibid.:4). Tension refers to "...whether a discourse reflects a struggle or polarization of some sort" (ibid.:6). Longacre's classification is used in Table 2.1 to contrast the characteristics of expository monologues with those of narratives.

Table 2.1. Characteristics of expository monologues & narratives.

	Expository monologues	Narratives
Chronological Linkage	-	+
Agent Reference	-	+
Projection	-/+	-/+
Tension	-/+	-/+

If one accepts that a narrative is "...the representation of at least two real or fictive events or situations in a time sequence..." (Prince, 1982), then it is clear that narratives are inherently characterized by +chronological linkage. In expository monologues, however, the "linkage" is logical or topical rather than chronological. Thus, expository monologues are characterized by –chronological linkage. Similarly, since the focus of narratives is always on an agent(s), or, more broadly, participant(s), narratives are characterized as +agent reference. In expository monologues, however, the focus is always on a theme or set of related themes with the use of other discourse types (e.g. narratives or jokes) functioning to introduce, clarify, or illustrate a theme. Certain categories of narratives (e.g. prophecies) and certain categories of expository monologues (e.g. proposing an economic plan), since they deal with actions that are contemplated or hoped for, are characterized by +projection. Other categories of narratives (e.g. historical biography) and expository monologues (e.g. linguistics lecture) have -projection. Finally, while certain types of narratives (which Longacre labels "episodic") are -tension and other types of narratives (which he labels "climactic") are +tension, expository monologues are

+tension. As Longacre (1982: 39) points out: "...an expository discourse of the better sort reflects a certain struggle, a struggle to achieve clarity in the face of recalcitrant elements in the subject itself and possibly in the lack of background on the part of those who are to hear the discourse."

Of these four characteristics, clearly the first, -chronological linkage, and second, -agent orientation, are most important, since they address the issues of the organization (logical or topical) and focus (thematic) of expository monologues. Thus, for purposes of the present study, it will be necessary to specify some of the textual strategies that are used to provide logical or topical organization and thematic focus in expository monologues. The formal, structural strategies for establishing logical/temporal organization and thematic focus within expository monologue can best be realized by examining the linguistic features used to create textual cohesion.

Textual Cohesion

Textual cohesion is a semantic concept that refers to relations of meaning that exist within a text (Halliday & Hasan, 1976). Since the focus of the present study is the interpretation of message (i.e. the cross-linguistic, cross-cultural transfer of meaning), the relevance of the linguistic indicants of cohesion is obvious. The following discussion draws heavily on the work of Halliday & Hasan (1976) who posit two general categories of cohesion: grammatical cohesion and lexical cohesion. Each of these categories can be sub-divided.

One type of grammatical cohesion is reference. Halliday & Hasan define reference as a case in which "...the information to be retrieved is the referential meaning, the identity of the particular thing or class of things that is being referred to; and the cohesion lies in the continuity of reference, whereby the same thing enters into the discourse a second time." (p. 31). There are two general ways in which referencing can be accomplished: (a) *exophoric* reference signals that reference must be made to the context of the situation, and (b) *endophoric* reference signals that reference must be made to the text of the discourse itself and is either anaphoric (reference to preceding text) or cataphoric (reference to following text).

Halliday and Hasan specify three types of reference: personal, demonstrative, and comparative. Personal reference in English is established by using nouns, pronouns, or determiners that refer, for example, to the speaker only ("I, me, my, mine"), the addressee with or without other persons ("you, your, yours"), other persons or objects ("they, them, their, theirs"), or an object or unit of text ("it, its"). Demonstrative reference is established by using determiners or adverbs that refer to locative or temporal proximity ("this, these, here"), locative or temporal distance ("that, those, there, then"), or are neutral ("the"). Comparative reference is established by using adjectives or adverbs that either express a general comparison based on identity ("some, identical, similar, additional"), or difference ("other, different, else"), or express a particular comparison ("better, more").

A second type of cohesion is substitution. Substitution takes two forms: substitution per se which is "...the replacement of one item by another" (p. 88), and ellipsis which is a form of substitution in which "...the item is replaced by nothing" (p. 88). The distinction between reference and substitution is that while reference is essentially a semantic relation or a relation between meanings, substitution is essentially a lexicogrammatical relation or a relation between linguistic units. A substitute is not an exact or identical replacement, however, since it contains information that differentiates it from the unit it replaces.

Halliday and Hasan identify three types of substitution: nominal, verbal, and clausal. Nominal substitution occurs when the substituted unit functions as a noun. Verbal substitution in English is accomplished by means of the lexical item "do" which can replace a verb or a verb plus other units. Clausal substitution is accomplished by using the lexical items "so" and "not". Nominal, verbal, and clausal ellipsis occurs when nouns, verbs, or clauses are replaced by nothing (or, colloquially, are omitted).

Lexical cohesion is created in a number of specific ways: the use of "general nouns" (which, since they are superordinate members of major lexical sets, function as a type of anaphoric synonym), reiteration of a lexical item (either the identical item, a synonym, or a superordinate), lexical collocation (all lexical cohesion not previous accounted for).

Using this discussion of expository monologues and cohesion, it is now possible to provide the analytic specificity that was lacking in the categorization of message-specific factors in Figure 2.1 Expansion of this portion of Figure 2.1 is given in Figure 2.2 on page 33.

Summary, Chapter 2

Expository monologue, the discourse genre that is of concern for this study, is outlined in Figure 2.2 . As has been noted above, interaction in expository monologues is non-reciprocal although the possibility for some reciprocity exists as in the case of questions during a lecture. In such a case one of two possibilities exist: either the discourse genre shifts to dialogue and the expected norms for expository monologues are suspended, or the intervening discourse genre is integrated into the expository monologue resulting in what Longacre (1982) calls a compound discourse. Since the focus of this study is not directly concerned with the issue of reciprocity, the data analyzed consist only of instances of nonreciprocal expository monologue.

The channel of expression of any expository monologue is, to some extent, determined by the relative proximity of the speaker/signer and addressee(s). In those cases where the expository monologue is to be delivered "face-to-face" the message will be spoken or signed and may or may not be amplified (e.g. through a microphone). In cases where the speaker/signer and addressee are not in physical proximity, the message may be written or pre-recorded. The primary distinction would seem to be that in the latter cases, the speaker/signer receives no feedback from the addressee(s) and there is no possibility for any immediate reciprocity or compound discourse.

The overall content of the message can be characterized by combinations of the features of projection and tension. While there are clearly formal indicants of these features, they would appear to be characteristic of the content of a message proper that are often, but need not be, formally encoded. The features linkage and reference, since they have specific, formal correlates, would appear to be characteristics of the form of a message rather than its content. More specifically, there are grammatical and lexical cohesion-forming elements that provide the logical/topical linkage and the thematic reference that are characteristic of expository monologue.

Figures 2.1 and 2.2 graphically illustrate those factors or considerations that shape and influence any communicative interaction and, as such, directly or indirectly influence the interpreter. What is crucial is that the interpreter must not only recognize these factors when they occur in the Source Language message, but must also identify and express Target Language correlates or equivalents for them. The extent to which the interpreter is able to accomplish this, with particular attention given to those form and content factors, will determine the accuracy or equivalence of the interpretation.

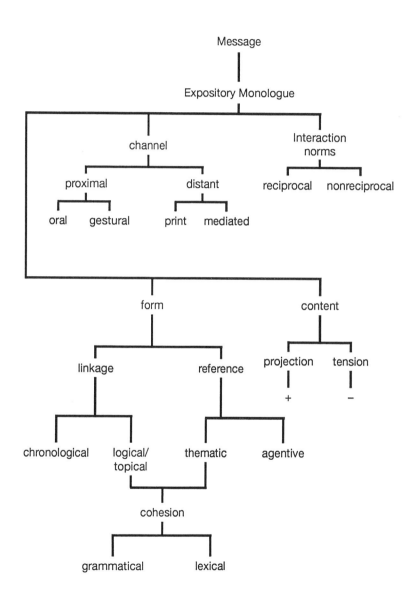

Figure 2.2. Further specification of message-specific factors.

CHAPTER THREE

OBTAINING A DATA BASE

The first step in developing a model of sign language interpretation is to collect data. Opportunity for this came during the winter of 1983, at the fourth national Conference of Interpreter Trainers (CIT) convention, held at the Asilomar Conference Center in Monterey, California. There were approximately 15 presentations during the convention, all of which were interpreted. Permission was obtained from speakers and interpreters to videotape ten of these presentations. Videotapes of interpreters were made using professional quality camera and recording equipment. An audio track of the speaker's presentation was simultaneously recorded on each videotape using a directional microphone.

For each presentation the camera focused on the interpreter so that the resulting video image was approximately three-fourths of a full body shot. Three-quarter-inch cassette duplicate work copies were made, with a digital display of hours, minutes, seconds, and tenths of seconds at the bottom of each tape.

Ten interpreters were videotaped in all. Of this number, six were selected for this study three with Deaf parents (DP) and three with Hearing parents (HP). Each of these interpreters had previously completed a questionnaire that provided basic demographic information. This background information is summarized in Table 3.1.

The average age of the total group at the time of the conference was 34.6 years (30.6 years for those with DP and 38.6 years for those with HP). The average number of years signing was 22.6 years (30 years for DP; 15.3 years for HP). Both groups had about the same paid interpreting experience (12.3 years for DP and 12.0 years for HP) and there was relatively little difference in the average length of time each group held certification from the Registry of Interpreters for the Deaf (9.0 years for DP and 7.6 years for HP).

Table 3.1. Interpreter characteristics.

	Int. 1	Int. 2	Int. 3	Int. 4	Int. 5	Int. 6
Gender	M	F	M	F	F	M
Age	30+	30+	25+	35+	35+	35+
Parents	DP	DP	DP	HP	HP	HP
Years Signing	31	33	26	21	11	14
Years Interpreting	11	18	8	16	10	10
Years Certified	9	11	7	10	3	10
Educational Level	BA+	MA+	BA+	BA+	MA+	MA+

None of the interpreters graduated from an interpreter preparation program, although two of them had taken courses in interpreting (Int. 3, 2 courses; Int. 5, 4 courses). All of the interpreters had extensive experience interpreting at conventions, conferences, and interpreting lectures and speeches. All of them had experience preparing interpreters or coordinating interpreting services.

While six interpreters were selected for this study, there were only four separate speakers for whom they interpreted. This is because one speaker gave two presentations and because two of the interpreters worked as a team to interpret one of those presentations. Thus, Int. 1, Int. 2, and Int. 4 interpreted for the same speaker. Furthermore, Int. 2 and Int. 4 interpreted the same presentation, relieving each other every twenty minutes.

All of the speakers were female. One of them had completed a doctorate and the other three were writing their dissertations. All of them had extensive experience teaching, conducting workshops and making presentations at professional meetings and conferences. All of the speakers were experienced at working with interpreters, and three of them are, in fact, themselves spoken language interpreters.

Each of the speakers provided the interpreters with a detailed outline or a completed version of her presentation in advance. In addition, the interpreters had the opportunity to meet with their respective speaker before the presentation. None of the speakers read from her paper. All made prepared, quasi-extemporaneous presentations. Only one of the speakers (Spk. 6) allocated time during the presentation and at the end for questions from members of the audience.

All of the presentations took place at the Asilomar Conference Center in Monterey, California, during the week of February 21, 1983. Specifically, the presentations occurred in a meeting facility known as "The Chapel" which is a separate building consisting of a single, large room (fixed seating capacity of 400) with three adjacent alcoves. There was a center aisle with two hundred seats on each side. In front of the room was a three-foot high stage approximately forty feet wide by fifteen feet deep. At the rear of the stage was a brown curtain or backdrop. A single podium was placed in the center of the stage with an overhead projector placed slightly to the right of the podium.

Interpreters were located at stage left (the audience's right). All but one of the presentations (Spk. 6) were also simultaneously transliterated. Transliterators were located at stage right (the audience's left) and, based on reports from the interpreters, could not be seen by the interpreters. Based also on reports from the interpreters, the presence of the transliterators served as a psychological reminder for the interpreters and an impetus for them to interpret and not to transliterate. That is, they reported that whatever they were doing at stage left had to "look more like interpretation" than what the transliterators, present at stage right, were doing.

The convention theme was "New Dialogues in Interpreter Education." This convention was the first organized attempt of the Conference of Interpreter Trainers to benefit from the evaluation, curriculum and preparation experiences of spoken language interpreter trainers. Each day of the convention was focused on a specific topic — curriculum design, simultaneous interpretation, consecutive interpretation, and evaluation. Each day began with a plenary session with a presentation on one of these topics. Three of the speakers in this study presented at these plenary sessions. The fourth speaker gave a theme-related paper although not at a plenary session.

All of the presentations can be categorized as expository monologues or lectures. In general each speaker discussed pertinent research, described her personal experiences *vis-a-vis* the particular topic, and offered practical suggestions for interpreter trainers.

There were approximately 150 convention participants, about 30 of whom were deaf. At the time of the convention, there were approximately 225 members of CIT. Membership in the CIT at that time was restricted to those who were directly or indirectly involved in interpreter preparation. The majority of the participants at the convention were affiliated with one of the then 80 sign language interpreter preparation programs nationwide. The majority of the participants (perhaps 75%) were female.

During all presentations most of the Deaf participants sat in the front section of seats. For the plenary sessions those Deaf people who chose to have the presentations interpreted (approximately 20) sat to the right (i.e. facing stage left) while those who chose to have the presentations transliterated (approximately 15) sat to the left (i.e. facing stage right).

While it is difficult to describe or document accurately the actual or perceived relationships between speakers and conference participants, there are some general observations that can be made. The biographical information on each speaker that was made available in the convention program and that was reiterated and expanded upon in the introduction of each speaker made it clear to all participants that these speakers could accurately be called "leading experts" in their respective fields. In addition, three of the speakers were outside the field of sign language interpretation. To the extent that "outsiders" are often accorded a greater degree of credibility than "insiders," this undoubtedly enhanced the participants' perceptions of these three speakers. The fourth speaker, although an "insider" in the field of Sign Language in general, may very well have been perceived by participants as an "outsider" in the field of interpreter preparation. In any event, this speaker's reputation is so well established that participants' perceptions of this speaker were likely at least equal to their perceptions of the other three speakers.

Selection of segments for analysis

The sheer quantity of videotaped data available on the six interpreters (more than 200 minutes) precluded transcription and analysis of the entire corpus. Consequently a sampling procedure was used that yielded twenty percent (20%) of the total tape time for each interpreter. The procedure consisted of selecting and transcribing the final minute of each five minute segment of tape available for each interpreter. While this procedure resulted in uneven sample sizes as noted in Table 3.2, there are several reasons why such a procedure seemed appropriate. First, it avoided having to select arbitrarily an equally long middle portion of each interpreter's performance that would not be influenced by sociolinguistic opening and closing behaviors. Second, even if selection of a medial portion of an interpreter's performance that was devoid of such behaviors on the speaker's part were possible, that segment might not necessarily be devoid of such behaviors on the interpreter's part. Third, the sampling used also avoided the possibility that other factors (e.g. a particular sub-topic within a presentation or a particular segment in which an interpreter produces a disproportionate number of miscues) might influence the selection process. Fourth, this procedure provided a more realistic indication of overall interpreter performance. The original quantity of tape available and the sample size selected using this procedure are given in Table 3.2.

Table 3.2. Selected sample sizes

	Int. 1	Int. 2	Int. 3	Int. 4	Int. 5	Int. 6
Total data: minutes	40	20	40	40	20	25
Sample size: minutes	8	4	8	8	4	5

Much of the subsequent discussion is presented in terms of percentage of each interpreter's total performance which allows comparison of interpreters' performance despite unequal sample sizes. In addition, subsequent chapters provide extrapolated values that, for comparative purposes, serve to equalize the sample size across interpreters.

When 3/4" cassette work copies of the videotapes with a digital display of hours, minutes, seconds, and tenths were complete, two native speakers of English transcribed and verified the audio portion only of each sample minute. A form was devised for recording these transcriptions to allow second-by-second synchrony of the transcriptions with the digital timing display on each tape. Ten seconds of a speaker's utterances were recorded per page.

Conventional orthography was used for speakers' utterances, as phonetic transcription would yield levels of information and data unnecessary for this study. Efforts were made, however, to ensure that certain phonetic phenomena (e.g. assimilation) could be reflected in the transcriptions. Consequently, the transcribers were instructed not to allow conventional spelling requirements to result in "transcription hypercorrections" of a speaker's utterances.

Transcribers of the sL audio had the option of listening to the audio track through the television monitor speakers or through headphones, which seemed to increase the audio fidelity. All verification was done using the headphones. In those cases in which the transcribers were unsure of what was said, they were instructed to indicate this clearly on the recording form so that during the verification stage particular attention could be given to those segments.

Transcribing the interpretations

Once the work copies were completed and the sample segments had been selected, a highly qualified and experienced Deaf native user of ASL did the original transcriptions of each interpreter's performance and, in conjunction with the author, verified those transcriptions. Transcriptions were recorded on a form identical to that used for the audio transcripts, thus enabling second-by-second synchrony with the digital timing display on each tape. Ten seconds of an interpreter's performance were recorded per page. At no time during the initial transcription stage was the transcription of a given sample minute of an interpreter's performance recorded on the form used to transcribe the speaker's utterances during that minute. In other words, the speaker's utterances and the interpreter's performance were independently transcribed and only after being verified were the two transcriptions placed on the same form.

As with the audio transcriptions, it was determined that a more phonetic-like transcription (e.g. Stokoe, 1965) would yield levels of information unnecessary for this study. Consequently, the transcription system detailed in Baker and Cokely (1980; see Appendix) was used. In general the conventions specify that a sign is recorded by using English words that attempt to indicate the meaning of that sign. The gloss for the sign is written in capital letters, and while it reflects one of the meanings of that sign, it obviously does not capture all possible meanings. In addition, the transcription conventions specify that co-occurring non-manual linguistic behaviors are to be written above the sign glosses on a line that extends for the duration of the particular non-manual behavior.

Transcription of interpreter performance was done using a JVC videorecorder (model CR-6600U) equipped with a remote control unit (model RM-70U) that makes possible forward and backward slow motion viewing and full stop with minimal distortion. Two color monitors were available for viewing the tapes (one 12" and one 19"). The smaller monitor was generally used to transcribe manual signs and the larger one was used to transcribe non-manual behaviors. As with the audio transcripts, instances of ambiguity were indicated clearly on the recording form so that during the verification stage particular attention could be given to those segments.

Transcription samples

To illustrate clearly the synchronized transcriptions after final verifications were completed, the transcript of twenty seconds of one sample minute is shown on the following pages. The number in the upper left-hand corner indicates the digital timing display at the beginning of this sample. Each triple slash (///) represents a new second. In those instances when a spoken word or sign overlapped these timing boundaries, hyphens were used to segment the word or the gloss. Hyphenation was not determined by syllabic constraints but was used to provide an approximation of the relative portions of the words or signs occurring on each side of the timing boundaries.

The sL message (i.e. speaker's utterances) appear on the topmost line. The second and third lines are used for the tL message (i.e. interpreter's utterances). The second line contains glosses for signs produced by the interpreter's dominant hand while the third line is for glosses for signs produced by the interpreter's non-dominant hand. Above the second line in parentheses or on a superscript line are the non-manual signals or behaviors of the interpreter.

Sample Transcriptions
4:01 — 4:10

Minute:Second	4:01	4:02
sL Message		area studies ///
Dominant hand and non-manual behaviors	(camera at screen ————) ///	———///
Non-dominant hand	///	///

4:03	4:04	4:05
		These courses ///
————/// ———) THAT ///	intense AREA	///
///	///	///

4:06	4:07	4:08
/// were taught ///	in the language ///
nodding nod	t
STUDY-lf /// THAT-lf ///	COURSE + , ///
INDEX-lf- ///	INDEX ——///

4:09	4:10
of the country /// that was being st- ///	
(body shift right- ————	
SUPPOSE YOU /// STUDY-wg SPECIFIC ///	
///	///

Sample Transcriptions
4:11 — 4:20

Minute:Second	4:11	4:12
sL Message	-udied	If I
Dominant hand and non-manual behaviors	(head shake)	///
	COUNTRY ANY	///
Non-dominant hand	///	5:CL↓

	4:13	4:14	4:15
	was studying	French history	These courses
		(b.r.) nod nod/cs	nod (head swing ←→)
	POSS (lh) LANGUAGE, INDEX /// YOU /// USE THAT ///		LANGUAGE (1h) TALKwg ABOUT ///
	5:CL ——————→ ///	5:CL ——————— ///	

	4:16	4:17	4:18
	would be tau-	-ght in French	
		(b.r. nodding)	
	THAT CO-	UNTRY YOU ///	IDEA "WELL"
		INDEX-lf -------- ///	

	4:19	4:20
	If I was st-	-udying
	(eyes up) nod	(b.r./nod)
	ME STUDYwg ABOUT FRANCE/// POSS CULTURE "WHOA"	

Quantitative temporal coding

After the audio and video transcripts were synchronized on the same recording forms, the data were first analyzed for the temporal char-acteristics of the texts. The results of this analysis are presented in Chapter 4. The initial step in this analysis consisted of identifying sentences and sentence boundaries in the sL text and then identifying sentences and sentence boundaries in the tL text. Intuitions of the transcribers were relied upon to make these identifications.

Once sL and tL sentences were identified, inter- and intra-text comparisons were possible. For example, onset time lag was determined by counting the number of seconds between initiation of a sL sentence and initiation of the tL sentence(s) that provided the interpretation of the source sentence. Temporal synchrony of sL and tL texts was determined by identifying the number of seconds in any sample minute during which there was total silence—either speaker silence, or interpreter silence. Thus, quantitative temporal analysis of the 20 seconds of data presented above would yield the following:

Table 3.3. Timing in sample transcriptions 4:01-4:20.

speaker silence:	5 seconds
interpreter silence	3 seconds
co-occurring silence	2 seconds
average onset time lag	3 seconds
Area studies	2 seconds
These courses...	2 seconds
If I was studying...	5 seconds

Qualitative linguistic analysis & semantic analysis

Once a sL sentence and the tL sentence(s) that provided the interpretation of that sentence were identified, each was analyzed syntactically and semantically at several different levels. Since one of the primary pieces of information in determining the accuracy of tL utterances is the information conveyed by the sL text, analysis of sL texts preceded analysis of tL texts. Each tL utterance, then, was analyzed with respect to the extent to which its meaning was equivalent to or different from that of the sL sentence. In addition, tL utterances were also analyzed with respect to the extent to which they conformed to the linguistic norms of ASL. Using the 20 seconds of data presented above as an example, it is possible to compare the sL and tL utterances and analyze information differences between them. It is also possible to analyze the tL utterances in terms of the extent to which they are syntactically acceptable in the tL.

The interpretation of the sL sentence initiated at 4:05 and ending at 4:11 begins at 4:07 and ends at 4:17 (*"These courses were taught in the language of the country that was being studied"*). With the sL message as the starting point, it is possible to determine how accurately the tL interpretation reflects the information conveyed by the sL. The sL plural (*"courses"*) is accurately conveyed by reduplication of the sign COURSE (COURSES+). The referent for *"These courses"* (i.e. *area studies*) was defined in the preceding context as providing a broad background of study in a country's history, civilization, and its political, social and economic systems. This extensive nature of area studies courses is not conveyed by "...(1h) TALK-wg ABOUT THAT COUNTRY..." It is also clear from preceding context that not all countries could or would be the object of such area studies courses. The interpretation, however, conveys the impression that these courses were much more extensive "...COUNTRY ANY...."

Even if it is momentarily assumed that the tL utterances from 4:07 4:17 are syntactically acceptable in ASL (although, in fact, they are not, as appears below), it is clear that certain information has been added to the sL message ("...COUNTRY ANY...") and that the tL lacks the specificity of the sL message ("...(1h)TALK ABOUT..."). In addition, the sL message specifies that these courses were taught in the particular language of the country being studied. To a native speaker of English, this implies that both teacher and students use the language. However, the tL interpretation does not convey this information nor is it possible to infer clearly that this is intended by the sL message. Thus, it is at best questionable whether the main point of the sL message ("using the language of a given country to study the various aspects of that country and its people") is accurately conveyed by the tL interpretation.

The interpretation of the sL sentence initiated at 4:12 and ending at 4:17 ("*If I was studying French history the course would be taught in French*") begins, apparently, at 4:17 and ends at 4:23 . Again, momentarily assuming syntactic acceptability in ASL, the tL interpretation clearly expands the intent of the sL message. This happens because of the use of a non-equivalent tL lexical item ("CULTURE"). Interestingly enough, there is a tL lexical item ("HISTORY") that would have accurately conveyed the sL meaning. This substitution of lexical items results in an expansion of the meaning and intent of the sL message. Again there is a lack of equivalence between sL and tL messages.

Syntactic Analysis

There are a number of syntactic irregularities in the interpretation of the initial sL sentence that render that interpretation syntactically unacceptable in the tL. Although the interpreter has manually indicated a conditional statement (4:09 - 4:12), the non-manual behaviors required to signal a conditional statement are absent. The result is that it is not clear that there is a conditional nor, even if one could deduce that there were, is it clear where the conditional ends and the consequence statement begins. In fact there is reason to believe that there is no clear conclusion or consequence to this manually indicated condition.

Another syntactic irregularity begins at 4:14. This portion of the interpreter's performance (4:14 - 4:16) is apparently a clear case of sL syntactic intrusion. Compare, for example, the interpreter's utterance at this point with the English "you use that language (to) talk about that country". If, in fact, the interpreter wished to convey this meaning (although given the discussion above, this meaning does not seem to accurately convey the sL intent) there are numerous options for doing so in the tL. None of these options involves such adherence to the syntactic structure of the sL. Interestingly, while this is clearly an instance of sL syntactic intrusion, it is not a case of sL message syntactic intrusion. That is, although it is clear that syntactic structures of the sL were used, these structures did not occur in the sL message. Another, less extensive example of sL intrusion occurs in 4:19.

Another possible source of syntactic difficulty stems from the fact that from 4:09 to 4:20 the interpreter uses only the neutral space in front of the body to produce signs. That is, referents are not "assigned" a spatial location to the interpreter's right or left. This means that in the tL message the referents for the two occurrences of the demonstrative pronoun "THAT"(4:14 and 4:16) are identical since the sign is produced in (or, more accurately, toward) neutral space. The interpreter's failure to "assign" a spatial location to "COUNTRY" (4:11) and "LANGUAGE" (4:14) undoubtedly contributes to the linearized tL utterance in 4:14-4:16. In fact, with the repetition of the lexical items "LANGUAGE" (4:15) and "COUNTRY" (4:16) the demonstrative pronoun would be referentially meaningless.

Miscue identification

Given the preceding discussion, it is apparent that identification of interpreter miscues involves answering two questions about any tL token. The first question is whether the information conveyed by the tL interpretation is the same as that conveyed by the sL message (i.e., is the interpretation accurate?). The second question is whether the information conveyed by the tL interpretation (accurate or not) is conveyed in a way that is in concord with the linguistic norms of the tL (i.e., is the interpretation acceptable in the tL?). Although these are posed as separate questions, they are, in fact, interrelated.

While the ideal situation would be a [+accurate, +acceptable] tL utterance, other combinations of accuracy and acceptability are possible. For example, it is possible to have a tL utterance that deviates from the sL message and is linguistically correct in the tL [-accurate, +acceptable]. It is also remotely possible to have a tL utterance that does not add to or omit information in the sL message but is linguistically incorrect in the tL [+accurate, -acceptable]. (Of course, the production of a linguistically incorrect or unacceptable tL utterance would, at the least, convey information about a person's linguistic competence. Assuming a linguistically correct sL utterance addition of this type of information might mean that such a tL utterance could be judged [-accurate].) Finally, it is possible to have a tL utterance that is neither accurate nor linguistically correct [-accurate, -acceptable].

The information conveyed by the sL message, then, is the semantic norm against which the information conveyed by the tL interpretation can be assessed. The linguistic norms of the tL is the syntactic norm against which the tL interpreted utterance can be assessed. Any tL utterance or portion of that utterance that results in a determination that the tL utterance in question is either [-accurate] or [-acceptable] will necessarily contain at least one miscue. While chapter 5 presents a detailed taxonomy of miscue types, there are some general statements that can be made about the ways in which tL utterances might be judged as either [-accurate] or [-acceptable].

There are three general ways in which the sL information can be inaccurately conveyed by the tL utterance. Information can be omitted in the tL utterance, information can be added to the tL utterance, or information can be substituted in the tL utterance. Any omission, addition, or substitution of information will necessarily result in a tL utterance that deviates to some degree from the information presented in the sL message. However, tL utterances containing omissions, additions, or substitutions are not inherently inappropriate or unacceptable tL utterances. Such tL utterances simply deviate to some degree from the intended meaning of the sL message.

Unacceptable tL utterances, for purposes of this study, fall into two general categories: sL intrusions and anomalies. sL intrusions are instances in which the tL utterance is conditioned by or influenced by the sL syntax and/or lexicon. While such utterances may be marginally intelligible to consumers, they are, nonetheless, unacceptable or inappropriate formulations of the tL. tL anomalies are utterances that are confused or meaningless in the tL. While it is conceivable that an intrusion miscue would not involve the omission, addition, or substitution of information, anomalies inherently do (unless, of course, the sL utterance is meaningless or confused. In such a case, however, a meaningless or confused tL utterance would be required to render an accurate equivalent of the sL message).

Miscues, therefore, are identified by the fact that they cause a difference in meaning between sL message and tL message and/or they cause the tL utterance to be syntactically unacceptable or inappropriate in the tL.

Summary, Chaper 3

Unlike previous studies of interpretation (e.g. Barik, 1972) that have been experimental in design, the data on which this study is based are not the result of a controlled experiment. They represent the actual behaviors of a group of interpreters interpreting for real consumers. The data collection procedures would seem to preclude conscious or unconscious attempts by the interpreters to skew their behaviors because of the presence of the video camera; that is, the interpreters were interpreting for the consumers, not for the camera. If there were any "camera effects" during the initial phases of a given interpreting assignment, it is unlikely that they could be sustained throughout the entire assignment (given the presence of the consumers). The 20% sampling procedure used not only minimizes the effects of such skewed behaviors, if any, but also ensures that a realistic sample of an interpreter's overall performance is obtained. In addition, the sampling procedure also serves to equalize the effects of opening and closing linguistic behaviors of both the speaker and the interpreter.

The procedure for identifying miscues involves not only determining whether the meaning of a given tL utterance deviates from the meaning of the sL message it is supposed to convey, but also determining whether that tL utterance conforms to the linguistic expectations of ASL. While there is a risk with such a procedure of counting a given miscue more than once (i.e. a tL utterance that deviates from the sL message might also be unacceptable in the tL), measures have been taken (cf. chapter 5) to avoid artificially inflating the actual occurrence of miscues.

CHAPTER FOUR

QUANTITATIVE TEMPORAL ANALYSIS

This chapter identifies certain temporal characteristics of the Source Language (sL) and Target Language (tL) texts and examines the degree of temporal synchrony between them. These temporal characteristics bear a direct relation to interpreter accuracy, as will appear in the following chapter.

Time labelling of the work copies possible made second-by-second transcription of the tapes. A native speaker of English made the audio transcripts. These transcripts were as complete as possible; i.e., they included false starts, abbreviations, mispronunciations, etc.

Speaker rates were calculated by counting the number of words uttered during each sample minute. The averages, words per minute (wpm), and words per second (wps), were then calculated for each speaker, giving "unadjusted" speaking rates. Because during any sample minute, the speaker is not engaged in speaking during each second, these rates were adjusted. Table 4.1. shows the "unadjusted" speaking rates. The average for the six speakers is 119.58 wpm, which is 44.7% slower than the unadjusted average conversational rate of 216.3 wpm reported for native speakers of English (Cokely, 1979).

Table 4.1. Unadjusted rates of sL speakers.

	Spk. 1	Spk. 2	Spk. 3	Spk. 4	Spk. 5	Spk. 6
wps	1.99	1.83	1.85	2.14	2.15	2.01
wpm	119.00	109.50	111.00	128.40	129.00	120.60

These unadjusted rates, calculated on the basis of a full 60 seconds, do not represent the actual rate at which the sL texts are presented. The actual rate of presentation can be calculated by extending the average number of words per minute only over the average number of seconds per minute that the speaker is actually engaged in speaking. That is, if pauses are eliminated, a more accurate notion of speaker rate can be obtained. Table 4.2 presents these adjusted speaker rates.

Table 4.2. Adjusted rates of sL speakers.

	Spk. 1	Spk. 2	Spk. 3	Spk. 4	Spk. 5	Spk. 6
wps	2.30	1.96	2.24	2.45	2.48	2.50
wpm	138.00	117.60	134.40	147.00	148.80	150.10

It should be noted that the rates presented in Table 4.2 are conservative rates, since pauses of less than one second were not removed from each sample minute. While this pause criterion is consistent with other timing studies (e.g., Hargreaves & Starkweather, 1959), shorter pause criteria ranging from 200 msec. (Boomer & Dittman, 1962) to 600 msec. (Barik, 1972) have also been used. Obviously the use of a shorter pause criterion would inflate the values given in Table 4.2.

The significance of the adjusted values given in Table 4.2 is that they represent the rates at which the sL texts are presented to the interpreters. That is, these values represent the "speech burst" rates of the sL texts between pauses of 1 second or longer.

Speaker pauses

The adjusted rates given in Table 4.2 are extrapolated rates, calculated as if there were no speaker pauses. However, since speakers do pause, it is necessary to examine the portion of each minute that speakers are engaged in speaking at the rates given in Table 4.2. The average speaking seconds (ss) and pause seconds (ps) per minute for each speaker and the relative percentage of time for each are provided in Table 4.3.

Table 4.3. Average speaking & pausing time.

	Spk. 1	Spk. 2	Spk. 3	Spk. 4	Spk. 5	Spk. 6
ss	51.56	55.75	49.50	52.38	52.25	48.20
%	85.93	92.92	82.50	87.30	87.08	80.33
ps	8.44	4.25	10.50	7.62	7.75	11.80
%	14.07	7.08	17.50	12.70	12.90	9.60

The figures in Table 4.3 better explain the differences between unadjusted and adjusted speaker rates. Speaker 1, for example, had an unadjusted rate of 119 wpm. However, those 119 words were uttered in 51.56 seconds. This means that the speaking rate was actually (119 divided by 51.56) 2.3 words per second, or 138 words per minute during those times that Speaker 1 was speaking. Adjusting speaker rates to account for pauses thus provides a more accurate indication of the speaker transmission rates with which interpreters must contend.

The relative proportions of speaking time and pausing time are of particular interest since it might be assumed that interpreters would take advantage of speaker pauses in order to deliver the interpreted message. Such a strategy would reduce the amount of time during which the interpreter is simultaneously engaged in listening to sL messages and delivering tL messages. As will be shown in the section on synchronization, this strategy does appear to be consciously employed by the interpreters.

An interesting question, but one which is outside the scope of this study, involves the relationship between speaker rate and proportion of speaking time. Speaker 6, for example, has the highest adjusted rate of transmission (150 wpm) and the lowest proportion of speaking time (80.33%). Speaker 2, on the other hand, has the lowest adjusted rate of transmission (117.6 wpm) and the highest proportion of speaking time (92.92%). If an index of information/message transmission could be calculated, it is possible that the difference between these two speakers would not be as great as it appears when one uses the simple index of words per minute. Thus, it is possible that both speakers convey approximately the same amount of information during a given minute. Speaker 6 might convey the information faster and hence need less time to convey the information than speaker 2, who, speaking at a slower rate, would require a greater portion of time to convey a similar amount of information. This, then, may account for the relatively similar interpreter rates noted below.

As was noted in the preceding chapter, the work copies of the videotapes were made with time encoding, which enabled a second-by-second transcription. All transcriptions of interpreter performance were done and verified by a native signer. Like the tL transcripts, these were also as complete as possible, included false starts, extraneous gestures, etc.

Interpreter rate

Interpreter rate was calculated by manually counting the number of signs produced per sample minute. The average signs per minute (spm) and signs per second (sps) were then calculated for each interpreter,[1] yielding "unadjusted" interpreting rates, since, during any sample minute, the interpreter is not engaged in signing during every second of that sample minute. Table 4.4 presents these "unadjusted" interpreting rates.

Table 4.4. Unadjusted interpreter rates

	Int. 1	Int. 2	Int. 3	Int. 4	Int.5	Int.6
sps	2.27	1.65	1.71	1.68	1.43	1.31
spm	136.00	99.00	102.60	100.90	85.80	78.40

These rates, as with the unadjusted speaking rates, do not represent the actual transmission rates of the tL text since pauses have not been eliminated. The adjusted interpreter rates are provided in Table 4.5. It is worth noting here that the average unadjusted rate of 100.45 spm represents a rate that is 40.2% slower than the unadjusted average rate of 168 spm reported for ASL conversations. This decrease (40.2%) is quite similar to the decrease from conversational rate (44.7%) noted for the speakers.

Table 4.5. Adjusted interpreter rates

	Int. 1	Int. 2	Int. 3	Int. 4	Int. 5	Int. 6
sps	2.33	1.71	1.92	1.89	1.57	1.57
spm	139.90	102.60	115.20	113.40	94.20	94.20

As with the adjusted Speaker rates, the adjusted Interpreter rates are conservative, because they are calculated using a minimum pause criterion of one second. The adjusted interpreter rates, then, represent the actual transmission rates at which the interpreted messages were delivered.

The adjusted rates given in Table 4.5 assume a "no pause" condition. However, since interpreters do pause, it is necessary to examine the proportion of signing time and the proportion of pausing time. Table 4.6 provides the average signing seconds (ss) and pause seconds (ps) per minute for each interpreter.

Table 4.6. Average signing & pausing time.

	Int. 1	Int. 2	Int. 3	Int. 4	Int. 5	Int. 6
sign seconds	58.30	57.75	53.62	53.25	54.75	49.80
%	97.17	96.25	89.37	88.75	91.25	83.00
pause seconds	1.70	2.25	6.38	6.75	5.25	10.20
%	2.83	3.75	10.63	11.25	8.75	17.00

While this information will be discussed in more detail in subsequent sections, it is worth noting that, in general, the proportion of signing time and pausing time is similar to the proportion of speaking time and pausing time reported in Table 4.3. Speakers were engaged in speaking an average of 86% of the total time and paused 14% of the total time while the interpreters signed an average of 91% of the total time and paused 9% of the time. This is consistent with previous research (Barik, 1972), which found that the interpretations of French-English interpreters exhibited speaking/pausing proportions that were generally similar to the speaking/pausing proportions of the speakers.

There is, however, an interesting question that arises at this point: how can one account for the fact that the interpreters are engaged in signing for a greater proportion of the time than the speakers are engaged in speaking?

While the scope of the present study does not directly address this question, there are a number of possible explanations that may account for this situation. It might be assumed, for example, that interpreters who are less experienced, or who are interpreting into their less familiar or second language (ASL), would use more signs, which would then result in a greater signing proportion. This assumption is not borne out by these data, which show that the more experienced interpreters (for whom ASL is a first language) not only sign a greater proportion of the time than those less experienced (for whom ASL is a second language) but also sign at a faster rate. Those interpreters with Deaf parents sign an average of 94.3% of the time at a rate of 2.12

spm while those with Hearing parents sign 87.7% of the time at 1.91 spm. It may well be that in order to interpret the sL message accurately and completely, interpreters simply need to use more signs, which would result in a greater proportion of signing time (depending on the rate at which the interpreter signs). It is most likely, however, that because larger body structures are involved in sign than in voice production, the time needed to produce signs is greater. In this case, the greater proportion of active time can be accounted for on the basis of physiological production factors.

Another factor (perhaps the most significant factor) that would result in an increased signing proportion has to do with the nature of simultaneous interpretation. Since the interpreter does not control the message content nor, in non-reciprocal situations, the development of that content, there is a certain element of uncertainty of expression that is associated with interpretation. As will be shown in the next chapter, this uncertainty may result in false starts, circumlocutions, simple lexical transliterations, and/or inappropriate interpretations that need to be repaired. Any of these behaviors will necessarily result in an increase in the proportion of signing time for the interpreter.

Temporal synchrony of sL & tL texts

The previous two sections examined the temporal characteristics of sL and tL texts as if they were separately produced. When considered separately, only two events or states are possible: speaking/signing or pausing. When the sL texts and tL texts are considered together, at any one time, then one of four events or states is possible: interpreter signing and speaker talking (s/t), interpreter signing and speaker pausing (s/-), interpreter pausing and speaker talking (-/t), or both interpreter pausing and speaker pausing (-/-). Table 4.7 presents the average number of seconds per minute for each of these events or states as well as the percentage of total time for each event or state.

Table 4.7. Temporal synchrony of sL & tL texts.

	Int. 1	Int. 2	Int. 3	Int. 4	Int. 5	Int. 6
s/t	50.00	53.50	45.87	47.13	48.25	39.80
%	83.33	89.17	76.45	78.54	80.42	66.30
s/-	8.30	4.25	7.75	6.12	6.50	10.00
%	13.84	7.08	12.92	10.21	10.83	16.66
-/t	1.56	2.25	3.63	5.25	4.00	8.40
%	2.60	3.75	6.05	8.75	6.66	14.00
-/-	0.14	0.00	2.75	1.50	1.25	1.80
%	0.23	0.00	4.58	2.50	2.09	3.00

If simultaneous interpretation were truly simultaneous (i.e., perfectly synchronized), then one would expect a greater degree of occurrence of the *s/t* condition and only minor occurrences of the *s/-* and *-/t* conditions. That this did not occur is an indication that interpreters may make use of the *s/-* and *-/t* conditions in order to obtain sufficient sL message units before producing an interpretation of those units (*-/t*). It is also an indication that interpreters use the *s/-* and *-/t* conditions to produce tL message units during periods when they are not simultaneously engaged in listening to the sL message (*s/-*).

Clearly the extent to which the *-/t* and *s/-* conditions occur is directly related to the extent of the interpreter's short term or working memory. Assuming omission-free interpretation, those interpreters with better developed short term memory skills are better able to use the *s/-* condition to render their interpretations without fear of omitting portions of the message and are able to engage in the *-/t* condition without fear of forgetting portions of the message. Time lag (or decalage) can provide a direct indicator of the interpreter's short term or working memory.

The s/- condition (interpreter signing, speaker pausing)

The information in Table 4.7 shows clearly that interpreters do make use of speaker pauses in order to deliver the interpreted message. The extent to which this strategy is employed can be seen by comparing total speaker pause time with the portion of that time during which the interpreter is signing (i.e., the **s/-** condition):

Table 4.8. Speaker pauses used by interpreters.

	Int. 1	Int. 2	Int. 3	Int. 4	Int. 5	Int. 6
Speaker pause secs.	8.44	4.25	10.50	7.65	7.75	11.80
s/- seconds	8.30	4.25	7.75	6.12	6.50	10.00
%	98.30	100.00	73.80	80.00	83.90	84.70

Of course this information does not indicate how speaker pauses are used by interpreters (e.g., whether for repairs or for paraphrasing). But it does show that during the major portion of the speaker pauses, interpreters are engaged in delivering some portion of the tL message. That interpreters make use of such a high percentage of speaker pauses (an average of 86.8%) would seem to provide support for the notion that this may well be a strategy that is consciously employed by interpreters and not simply a function of using those pauses to "catch up" with the speaker. Certainly such a strategy, when appropriately coupled with the -/t condition, can reduce the cognitive demands on the interpreter. By increasing the portion of time that s/he is engaged in only one of two activities (delivering the tL message or listening), the interpreter is thereby able to decrease the total time that s/he must be engaged in both activities simultaneously.

The -/t condition (interpreter pausing, speaker talking)

The -/t condition is that portion of sL message time that the interpreter is not simultaneously engaged in signing. Presumably the interpreter is listening to the sL message (and presumably attempting to determine the meaning and appropriate interpretation of that message). By comparing the total interpreter pause time with the portion of that time during which the speaker is talking (the **-/t** condition), it is possible to determine the extent to which the interpreter is engaged in listening to the sL message without simultaneously having to interpret a portion of the sL message.

Table 4.9. Interpreter listening time

	Int. 1	Int. 2	Int. 3	Int. 4	Int. 5	Int. 6
Int. pauses	1.70	2.25	6.38	6.75	5.25	10.20
-/t secs.	1.56	2.25	3.63	5.25	4.00	8.40
%	91.80	100.00	56.90	77.80	76.20	82.40

Of course this information does not indicate that the interpreter was, in fact, listening to the speaker during the -/t condition. Rather it indicates the amount of time during which it was possible for the interpreter to be listening without simultaneously having to produce a tL message. That the portion of total interpreter pause time during which the -/t condition obtains is so high (an average of 80.9%) would again seem to argue that it is a strategy consciously employed by the interpreters. Intuitively and linguistically this strategy would seem appropriate since the accuracy of the tL message is influenced by the extent to which the interpreter understands the sL text. The extent to which interpreters can wait before beginning to deliver the tL message (as partially indicated by the -/t condition) is, of course, directly related to the interpreter's time lag which will be discussed in the next section.

The -/- condition (interpreter not signing, speaker silent)

Given the cognitive demands of simultaneous interpretation, it is worth noting that, depending upon how the interpreters make use of speaker pauses, there is very little time when they are not engaged in some activity. The only cognitive respite can occur during the -/- condition (although it could be argued that even during such times the interpreter is engaged in trying to predict or anticipate the next portion of the sL message). The brevity of condition -/- (an average of 1.2 seconds per minute) underscores the demands of simultaneous interpretation. It is little wonder then that after twenty minutes interpreters become fatigued and the likelihood of errors increases (Brasel,1976).

Of course, interpreters could increase the duration of the -/- condition by reducing the s/- and -/t conditions and increasing the s/t condition. However, to do so would force interpreters into a situation where they would not be able to use the tL. Rather they would be forced to use the sL syntax and merely substitute tL lexical items according to sL structural constraints. Clearly such a situation would place additional cognitive demands on consumers who may not know the sL or for whom the sL may be a second language. Not only would they be expected to comprehend the content of the sL message but they would also be forced to decode incoming messages with syntactic structures that they may not be familiar with or understand. The very reason that interpreters are employed is to allocate and distribute cognitive tasks to let consumers devote undivided attention to message content without having to struggle with sL message form.

Time lag: interpreter lag time

As should be evident by now, interpreters cannot (and do not) immediately begin interpreting at the very moment the speaker begins uttering the sL message. Interpreters must wait until they have heard a sufficient portion of the sL message in order begin to producing the tL rendition. This period of time between sL perception and tL rendition is the interpreter's *time lag* or decalage.

Average time lags ranging from 2-3 seconds (Barik, 1972) to 10 seconds (Oleron & Nanpon, 1965) have been reported and are largely a function of the structural differences between the sL and the tL. When the structures (i.e.,ordering of lexical items) of the two languages are similar, a shorter lag time is possible. When the structures are significantly different, a longer lag time is required. Of course when working with two languages that are structurally different, the interpreter must maintain a suitable time lag not only to allow appropriate tL structures to be used but also not to overtax the limits of short term or working memory, thereby increasing the likelihood of omissions.

Onset lag time

Onset lag time in the present data was determined by calculating the time between the onset of a sL sentence and the onset of the tL interpretation of that sentence. Thus, onset lag time can provide a general indication of how much sL information the interpreter receives before beginning the tL interpretation. Table 4.10. provides the average onset time lag for each interpreter, the time lag range and the number of sL sentences used to calculate this time lag.

Table 4.10. Average onset time lag in seconds.

	Int. 1	Int. 2	Int. 3	Int. 4	Int. 5	Int. 6
Total sL sentences	34.00	19.00	30.00	44.00	22.00	27.00
Range in seconds	1-5	1-6	1-4	1-6	1-6	4-8
Ave. lag in seconds	2.40	3.00	1.70	2.40	2.70	4.80

If the average lag times reported in Table 4.10. are compared with the adjusted speaker rates in Table 4.2., it is possible to obtain a more accurate indication of how much sL information each interpreter obtains before interpreting. In other words, it is possible to calculate the sL input received as a function of lag time. Table 4.11. presents the minimum and maximum sL input based on each interpreter's lag time range and average lag time.

Table 4.11. Source Language input as a function of lag time.

	Int. 1	Int. 2	Int. 3	Int. 4	Int. 5	Int. 6
Speaker rate (wps)	2.30	1.96	2.24	2.45	2.48	2.50
Minimum sL input (wds.)	2.30	1.96	2.24	2.45	2.48	10.00
Maximum sL input (wds.)	11.50	11.80	8.96	14.70	14.80	20.00
Average sL input (wds.)	5.50	5.90	3.80	5.90	6.70	12.00

As will be shown in chapter 6, one of the primary causes for mis-interpretations appears to be the lack of sufficient sL input. That is, an interpreter's ability to select appropriate tL structures and appropriate tL lexical items is directly influenced by the amount of sL text available to that interpreter. The amount of sL text available at any given time is, of course, determined by the interpreter's lag time. The shorter the lag time, the greater the probability of inappropriate tL syntactic structures and of inappropriate tL lexical choices and the greater the probability that the interpreter will adhere to the sL syntax (i.e., provide a literal translation). Conversely, the longer the lag time, the greater the probability of rendering an interpretation that is syntactically and lexically appropriate in the tL (assuming that the greater lag time does not result in omissions and, of course, assuming tL competence on the part of the interpreter).

Medial & terminal lag time

Previous studies of simultaneous interpretation have calculated overall lag time in such a way that it is not possible to discern clearly differences between onset, medial, and terminal lag times. In these studies, the number of "words lagged behind" was calculated at five-second intervals (Treisman, 1965), or the amount of "time lagged behind" was calculated at five-second intervals (Barik, 1972). With either measure, differences in onset, medial, and terminal lag times are not evident. In attempting to calculate medial and terminal lag times, however, it becomes evident that these lag times can only be rather arbitrarily arrived at and, indeed, are not as meaningful nor as crucial as onset lag time.

Assume, for the moment, that it is desirable to calculate the overall lag time for the following sentence: "I'm going skiing if it snows tomorrow." In order to render this sentence appropriately, the interpreter cannot start until the speaker has uttered the full sentence (because in ASL the conditional portion would normally be signed first). Assuming that the speaking rate is 2.3 wps (the average rate of the speakers in this study), it would take approximately 3 seconds to utter the sentence. If the interpreter produced the following tL message:

_____cond
#IF TOMORROW SNOW, ME GO-TO-rt SKI

the interpretation would also take 3 seconds at a rate of 1.8 sps (the average rate of the interpreters in this study). Assume that the sampling period has been set at 3 seconds (instead of 5 seconds) and at that point we attempt to calculate the "number of words lagged behind," following Treisman (1965). Since the word uttered at the sampling point was "tomorrow," we would look for this lexical item in the interpretation. Since the sign TOMORROW would be the second sign produced, we would conclude that the interpreter was less than one second behind the speaker. If we then averaged the onset and terminal lag times (3 seconds and 1 second respectively) we would arrive at a lag time of 2 seconds.

Clearly, however, such a procedure fails to account for any re-structuring of information that the interpreter may have done because of the tL syntax, or may have been able to do because of a longer onset time lag. While it is possible that such a procedure may be valid for languages that are somewhat structurally similar (e.g. English and French, the languages in the Treisman and Barik studies), it cannot yield meaningful time lag results for structurally dissimilar languages like as English and ASL. In addition, such a procedure cannot properly account for interpreter omissions or difficulties and delays, since these would have the net effect of decreasing and increasing overall lag time respectively.

Given the limitations mentioned above and the lack of an appropriate metric for determining medial and terminal lag times, no such calculations have been attempted in this study. Even if it were possible to calculate these lag times with some accuracy, it is not clear that they would be more meaningful than onset lag time.

Pausing, non-pausing & lag times

In examining the temporal characteristics of sL and tL texts, there are several observations that will be relevant for subsequent qualitative analysis of these texts. These observations are summarized below.

When one compares the percentage of speaking/pausing time with the percentage of signing/pausing time, there are only slight differences (86%/14%, and 91%/9%, respectively). At least in this regard, then, the interpreted texts are generally produced within certain temporal parameters determined by the sL text. The lack of temporal studies of ASL in similar formal situations makes it impossible to determine the extent to which the signing/pausing times of the interpreters in this study represent expected ASL signing/pausing times. While it is possible that these signing/pausing times would compare favorably with expected ASL times, it is also possible that they would be quite different. It may very well be that cultural and/or linguistic differences would necessitate different pausing and non-pausing proportions. The interpreter, then, constrained by the temporal characteristics of the sL text, may be compelled to mirror more closely the pausing/non-pausing expectations of the sL. This would have definite implications if one were to focus on the overall comprehension and comfort of those consumers who are dependent upon the tL interpretation of the sL text.

Although the general proportion of signing/pausing time is similar to the speaking/pausing time, it is worth noting that in all instances the interpreters are engaged in signing a greater portion of the time than their respective speakers are engaged in speaking. This may be due, in part, to the difference between the articulation time needed for words and the production time needed for signs. It may also reflect a certain hesitancy on the part of the interpreters, who are dependent upon the speakers for the content of the message. In the case of Interpreter 1, however, the greater proportion of signing time can be at least partially accounted for by the fact that, unlike the other interpreters, this interpreter produces more signs per minute than the speaker produces words per minute. This greater verbosity on the part of Interpreter 1 will force the interpreter to be engaged in signing a greater portion of the time (assuming that, as in this case, the interpreter does not significantly increase signing rate).

That other studies have also noted a greater portion of interpreting time when compared with speaking time (e.g., Barik, 1972) may indicate that this is a constant and expected condition for simultaneous interpretation. Similar comparisons of interpreting time and speaking time for consecutive interpretation would reveal whether this condition is constant for interpretation per se or an artifact of simultaneous interpretation.

The use of pauses

The data support the suggestion that interpreters try to make use of speaker pauses in delivering the tL interpretation. The fact that approximately 87% of all speaker pauses are used by the interpreters would seem to indicate that this is a conscious strategy on the part of interpreters. Presumably the motivation for using speaker pauses is to reduce the portion of time during which the interpreter must simultaneously decode and encode different messages.

The data also support the suggestion that interpreters use their own pauses to reduce the portion of time that they must simultaneously decode and encode different messages and, when these pauses occur while the sL message is being delivered, to better understand the sL message. The extent to which interpreters can use their own pauses for these purposes is presumably directly dependent upon the capacity of their short term or working memory.

The data on pausing reveal that very few interpreter pauses coincide with speaker pauses. Since interpreters make use of a large portion of speaker pauses, this is not surprising. The result, however, is that there is virtually no time when the interpreter is not engaged in some aspect of the simultaneous interpretation process. The cumulative effects of this level of cognitive and—in the case of English-ASL interpretation—physical activity upon interpretation accuracy have not been thoroughly documented. However, it is clear that among the cumulative effects is the increased likelihood of fatigue-induced errors.

Lag time

The average onset lag time for the interpreters in this study is 2.8 seconds. Since there is a direct relationship between comprehension of the sL message and interpretation accuracy, it is reasonable to expect that those interpreters who are able to receive more of the sL message before delivering the tL interpretation will provide consistently more accurate inter-pretations. Conversely, one would expect an increase in false starts, repairs, intrusions, and errors on the part of those interpreters who deliver the tL interpretation prematurely, with shorter lag times. (That this seems to be the case will be demonstrated in the next chapter.)

Evidence that a 2-3 second time lag does not represent a time lag ceiling (nor, possibly, an optimum time lag for English-ASL interpretation) is provided by the performance of Interpreter 6. The average time lag exhibited by this interpreter (4.8 sec.) is exactly twice the average time lag for the other five interpreters (2.4 sec.).

Even the shortest time lag for Interpreter 6 (4 sec.) exceeds the average lag time of the other interpreters by 66%. Clearly all of the interpreters are capable of greater lag times as evidenced by the upper limits of their time lag range. The fact that, in general, they function at the lower end of this range raises some interesting questions for future research and has definite implications for preparation and, broader, educational programs for students of interpretation.

It is also worth noting that interpreter time lag does not seem to be determined or influenced by speaker rate. Interpreter 6, with the longest time lag, interpreted for the speaker with the highest adjusted speaking rate. Interpreter 2, with the second longest lag time, interpreted for the speaker with the lowest adjusted speaking rate. Interpreter 3, with the shortest lag time, interpreted for a speaker whose rate was approximately the average of all speakers. Thus, it does not seem to be the case that higher speaking rates necessarily result in longer lag times.

Summary, Chapter 4

The results of the temporal analysis of sL and tL texts allow certain generalizations to be made about interpreter performance. Interpreters are engaged in signing for a greater portion of time than speakers are engaged in speaking, although the general proportion of signing/pausing time does not appear to differ significantly from the proportion of sL speaking/pausing time. Interpreters do make use of speaker pauses to deliver the tL interpretation and also make use of their own pauses to better understand the sL message. Since interpreter pauses generally do not co-occur with speaker pauses, the cognitive demands on the interpreter are virtually constant during the entire duration of the interpreting assignment. Among these demands is the need to lag behind the sL message to comprehend the sL message before producing the tL rendition of that message. Typically the average lag time is at the lower end of the range of lag times exhibited. There does not, however, appear to be any causal relation between speaker rate and lag time.

These generalizations confirm previous temporal studies of simultaneous interpretation and provide the basis for a number of systematic investigations of the temporal characteristics and factors influencing simultaneous interpretation. For example, the locus of speaker and interpreter pauses and the extent to which interpreter signing/pausing time represents tL expectations are two areas that warrant further study. The extent to which the temporal characteristics of sL and tL texts, more specifically, interpreter time lag, influence the quality and accuracy of the interpretation are discussed, in part, in the next chapter.

[1] There is no standard procedure for calculating number of signs per minute. Since spm and sps are not directly compared with wpm and wps, relative rate comparisons between interpreters are possible so long as the same criteria are applied to each interpreter. The count used here to calculate interpreter signing rate is as follows: a count of 1 for single sign, each repetition, a number, a sign modulation, a nonmanual signal alone, a contraction, a compound sign, a fingerspelled word (<1sec.); 2 for two signs produced simultaneoulsy, a partial contraction, fingerspelled word (>1sec.).

Obviously changes could be made in these criteria which would affect the calculation of signing rate. For example, counting simultaneously produced signs as one unit or contractions as two units would decrease and increase the calculations respectively. While such adjustments would influence the calculations, it is unlikely they would significantly alter the relative comparisons reported here.

CHAPTER FIVE

QUALITATIVE LINGUISTIC ANALYSIS

For an interpretation to be considered accurate or appropriate, the meaning of the source language message must be determined by the interpreter and conveyed in such a way that that meaning is intelligible in the target language. The very nature of the interpreting process makes it possible to determine accuracy or appropriateness by comparing the interpreted tL text with the source language text it is supposed to convey. Comparison and analysis of both sL and tL texts makes it possible to determine the extent to which interpreted text tokens adhere to or deviate from the meaning of their sL text counterparts. Such an approach is somewhat related to that used in identifying miscues in reading (Goodman and Burke, 1972) which are then used to examine the interaction between the language of the reader and the language of the author.

Comparison of sL and tL texts will necessitate an accurate understanding of the meaning of the sL text and the syntactic devices used to convey that meaning, as well as an accurate understanding of the meaning of the tL text and the syntactic devices used to convey that meaning. Only then is it possible to determine the extent to which equivalence in meaning has been achieved in the tL text. Those instances in which equivalence is not achieved can be considered miscues - i.e. deviations from the original text.

Miscues thus identified can be categorized and quantified according to type of miscue and according to likely cause(s) or motivation(s) for the miscue. While it is often difficult to deduce or attribute cause for interpreter miscues (since frequently there may be more than one plausible causal explanation) it is precisely this information that will reflect the various stages in the interpretation process. Since interpretation is a process, when breakdowns or miscues occur they will do so at major stages or critical points in the process. Categorization of miscues and miscue causes will provide direct evidence of the major stages in the interpretation process.

General miscue types

A miscue has been defined as a lack of equivalence between the sL message and its interpretation or, more specifically, a lack of concordance between the information in an interpretation and the information in the sL message it is supposed to convey. There are five general ways in which the tL message may deviate from the sL message: omissions, additions, substitutions, intrusions, and anomalies.

Omissions. Information contained in the sL message may be left out of the tL message. For purposes of this study sL message information will not include sL false starts, irrelevant repetitions, and vocalized pauses (e.g., "ya know"). However, it must be recognized that these sL speaker behaviors may serve a crucial function in allowing consumers to form affective judgments about the speaker. As such, equivalent tL behaviors should be provided by the interpreter in order to enable those dependent on the interpreter to form accurate affective judgments about the speaker (Cokely, 1983). Also, this category will not include the exclusion of material due to other types of miscues (e.g. substitution miscues which could be viewed as the omission of certain information and the addition of other information in its place).

Additions. Information that has no corollary in the sL message may be added to the interpretation . As with omissions, the count of tL information will exclude interpreter false starts, irrelevant repetitions, etc. Again, however, the role of these behaviors in influencing comsumers' affective judgments about the speaker must not be overlooked. Also this category will not include the addition of new information that arises because of other types of miscues (e.g. substitution).

Substitutions. Information contained in the sL message may be replaced by information in the interpretation that is at variance with the intent of the sL message. The substituted sL information may consist of the meaning of a single lexical item or may consist of the meaning of an entire sentence.

Intrusions. Source language syntactic structures or lexical collocations may be used in the interpretation that result in a transliteration of the sL message rather than an interpretation of that message. Although it may be argued that intrusions are basically substitutions, intrusions are inappropriate and unacceptable tL utterances identifiable by their adherence to the syntax and lexical semantics of the sL. Substitutions, on the other hand, are syntactically and lexically acceptable tL utterances that convey information different from that conveyed by the sL message.

Anomalies. The interpretation may also contain or consist of target language utterances that are meaningless or confused and that cannot be reasonably accounted for by another miscue type.

Previous discussions of the possible ways in which an interpreted text could deviate from its sL text (e.g. Gerver, 1969; Barik, 1972) have focused on omissions, additions, substitutions, and anomalies. Lexical and syntactic intrusion have generally been viewed as instances of substitution. To do so, however, arbitrarily inflates the substitution category and ignores what is, intuitively and linguistically, a different type of miscue. In addition, the historic lack of distinction between sign language

interpretation and transliteration argues for separate identification of intrusions (i.e. transliterations) as one means of
disambiguating the two. (Conversely, if one were studying
transliterator miscues it might be appropriate to establish a
miscue category of "interpretations").

Each of the five categories of miscues will be further refined by
detailing the miscue domain (lexical, syntactic, or semantic) and
the relative severity of the miscue (the extent to which the sL
message can be deduced from or recovered from the tL miscue).
While the first three categories of miscues address the content
equivalence between interpretation and sL message, they do not
indicate the extent to which the tL interpreted message is an
acceptable utterance in the tL. It is possible, for example, for an
interpretation to commit one or more of these types of miscues but
still be a grammatically correct tL utterance. Such an utterance
would be inappropriate but acceptable. Other combinations of
appropriateness and acceptability are also possible. Thus, it will
be necessary to indicate whether a given tL utterance is
acceptable, unacceptable, or questionable according to the
syntactic structures of ASL.

Of course, in identifying miscue types, the major concern is the
degree to which the interpretation is equivalent to the sL message,
not the degree of "cleverness" or "elegance" with which the
interpretation was rendered. Therefore, distinctions between
acceptable and unacceptable tL utterances must be made solely on
the basis of conformity to the syntax of the tL, not on the basis of
aesthetics. It is conceivable that the category of acceptable tL
utterances could be further refined on the basis of stylistics or
aesthetics. However, such refinements are outside the scope of
this study.

Omissions

As mentioned above, this category of miscues refers to instances in
which lexically conveyed sL information has been left out of the tL

interpretation. This miscue category has been sub-divided in order to reflect to some degree the sL levels of information that may be conveyed.

Morphological omission refers to the omission of content information that is clearly conveyed by bound morphemes in the sL message. A frequently occurring type of morphological omission involves plurals in the sL message; e.g.:

> **sL**: "*... for the Russian teachers...*"

>   <u>body shift to left</u>
> **tL**: "...   TEACH AGENT RUSSIA......"
>   INDEX-rt

> **Back translation of tL**: '... the teacher of Russian...'

The information conveyed by the plural *-s* has been omitted. Had the interpreter signed "...INDEX-*sweep*-rt.... " or had the location to the interpreter's right been previously designated as a group (of teachers), then the information conveyed by the bound morpheme *-s* would not have been omitted. Failure to do so means that the tL message must be understood to apply to only a single teacher of Russian.

Lexical omission refers to the omission of content information that is clearly conveyed by distinct (non-grammatically cohesive) lexical items or phrases in the sL message. While there is no expectation for a one-to-one correspondence between sL lexical items and tL lexical items, nevertheless the information conveyed by sL lexical items must be appropriately accounted for in the tL message; e.g.:

sL: "*What do I mean by these policy decisions?*"

nod	brow squint	tl
tL: " POLICY	MEAN #WHAT	"WELL" ..."

Back translation of tL: 'Policy means what? Well...'

The information conveyed by *decisions* has been omitted. While it can be argued that POLICY necessarily implies that antecedent action has occurred (i.e. policy decisions have been made), it is clear that the focus of the sL message is on the decisions that must be made that will result in policy, and not, as the interpretation implies, on the policy itself. The tL message focuses on product or outcome; the sL message focuses on process.

Cohesive Omission refers to the omission of the informational and/or functional value of an item in the sL text that can only be determined by reference to or relation with a preceding item in the sL text. While cohesion can be both lexical and grammatical, this subcategory will apply only to instances of omission of grammatically cohesive items, since omissions of lexically cohesive items (e.g. pronouns) are treated as instances of lexical omission; e. g.:

sL: "...*more or less matching what the matrix told us we wanted. Then we started refining that* (the test)..."

‾‾‾‾‾‾‾‾‾‾‾‾‾‾‾‾‾t

tL: "...(2h) THAT GOAL APPROACH , If-SAME-AS-rt
(eyes head rt.   )
SCHEDULE $_{THAT}$ HONORIFIC-rt,

‾‾‾‾t

NOW ALMOST If-SAME-AS-rt, (IHR)   ME,

START CHANGE++ R-E-F-I-N-E CHANGE+++..."

Back translation of tL: "... approaching that goal? It is like the matrix here. Now (?) is almost the same as the matrix. Me? I started changing, refine, changing (something)...

The information conveyed by *Then* and *that* in the second sentence have been omitted. While it is possible that the juxtaposition of sentences may make it possible to infer the temporal sequence of the sL message, it is more probable that sequentiality would not be inferred since appropriate means of signaling temporal sequentiality in the tL are absent. In the case of the sL demonstrative ("that"), the meaning of the tL interpretation is ambiguous at best. It might be thought that the tL items "...CHANGE++ R-E-F-I-N-E CHANGE+++..." refer to "... SCHEDULE $_{THAT}$ ..." since the spatial location (neutral space) is the same for both. However, if this were the case, the items "...CHANGE++ R-E-F-I-N-E CHANGE+++..." would have been produced at or toward the interpreter's right, because the interpreter has, in fact, specified a location for "...SCHEDULE ... "(by virtue of the signs "...THAT-rt. . . HONORIFIC-rt..."). Two other meanings are possible: 'both the text and the matrix were changed' or 'something unspecified or yet to be specified was changed.' Either meaning is, obviously, quite different from that conveyed by the sL message.

Additions

This category of miscues refers to information which appears in the tL message but which does not appear in the original sL message. This miscue category has also been sub-divided to reflect different types of tL addition of information.

Non-manual Additions are nonmanual signals that co-occur with manual signs which convey information in the tL message different from the intent of or information conveyed by the sL message. This subcategory will be restricted to those nonmanual signals that function as adverbs or modifiers ('mm', 'cs', 'th', 'puffed cheeks', 'pursed lips', and 'intense') and are co-terminus with manually produced signs; e.g.:

> **sL:** "... *an analogy to the simultaneity of listening and speaking in simultaneous* (interpretation)..."

>   th
> **tL:** "...(2h) 1-CL 'parallel' (1) SAME IDEA RECEIVE-THRU-EAR ——— ..."
>   1———————————————   TALK—

> **Back translation of tL:** '...a parallel, similar idea (to) inattentive listening and carelessly talking simultaneously...'

In this instance the nonmanual adverb 'th'adds the meaning 'carelessly'or 'without paying attention' to the tL manual signs RECEIVE-THRU-EAR and TALK. Clearly the resultant meanings ("to listen inattentively" and "to talk carelessly") are not motivated by nor in harmony with the sL message. In some cases, it is possible that certain signs and particular nonmanual behaviors have been learned by or are perceived by interpreters as single items. If this is the case, then the specific nonmanual behavior would be produced automatically whenever the sign is produced, whether that nonmanual behavior is semantically appropriate or not.

Lexical addition refers to lexical items in the tL message which add information to the sL message. This sub-category is restricted to the addition of information and obviously does not include, for example, those instances in which the interpreter may make explicit certain cases of endophoric reference: e.g.:

> **sL:** "... *If I was studying French history the course would be taught in French...*"

          (eyes up)   <u>nod</u>
tL: "IDEA ME   STUDYwg ABOUT ERANCE POSS CULTURE

<u>brow raise/nod</u>   (body shift lft)   <u>nod</u>
"WHOA",   ME WILL   (2h)TALKwg FRANCE
                                       (brow raise)
                                      <u>(nodding)</u>
DURING ME TEACH (1h)THAT INDEX-rt "WELL"——

> **Back translation of tL:** 'Idea I study about France, its culture umm I will French while I teach that ? umm...'

All the following has been added: ME WILL (2h)TALKwg...DURING ME TEACH. In this instance, although the sL message does not specify who will teach the course, it is clear that the speaker has hypothetically assumed the role of student. In the interpretation, however, not only has the teacher been specified, but the speaker has been given that role by the interpreter. The passive voice construction of the sL message probably motivated the interpreter to specify an actor. However, the use of a more "neutral "lexical item (e.g. TEACH-AGENT) would have been more faithful to the sL message. Clearly the specification of speaker as actor/teacher is information added to the sL message.

Cohesive addition refers to the addition of an item(s) in the tL text that establishes reference or a relation with preceding tL message units that did not exist in the sL message. This sub-category is

restricted to the addition of grammatical cohesive-creating units,
since lexical cohesive-creating units are treated as instances of
lexical addition; e.g.:

sL: "...*The second task is always designed to distract students'attentio*
from the primary task. An analogy to the simultaneity (of listening
and talking)..."

(body tilt rt)
tL: ... OTHER WORK MUST POINT---OFF-THE-POINT PERSON

_____ th
INTERPRET-AGENT If-SHIFT-FOCUS-TO-cntr

_____intense nodding   nodding
MUST INDEX-middle finger   THING,   BECAUSE WANT

(2h)1-CL 'parallel' (1h)SAME IDEA ..."
   1————————————————

Back translation of tL: '...other task must specify--digress, person
interpreter must carelessly shift attention to [the] second thing
because I want [a] parallel, similar idea ...'

The interpreter has added BECAUSE so that the interpretation
posits a causal relationship which has not been specified in the sL
message. In the sL message the function and purpose of the
"second task" is to provide a distraction from the primary task.
The fact that the second task functions as a distractor provides a
situation that happens to be analagous to the simultaneity of
listening and speaking that is encountered in simultaneous
interpretation. In the interpretation, however, the posited reason
for the existence of the "second task" is precisely because of the
desire to create a situation analagous to that encountered in
simultaneous interpretation. Thus, the interpretation adds a level
of grammatical cohesion that does not exist in the sL message.

Substitutions

This category of miscues refers to instances in which information contained in the sL message has been replaced by information in the interpretation that is at variance with the intent of the sL message. It is possible to argue theoretically that all tL deviations from the sL message are cases of substitution (e.g. omission = replacement of sL items by "nothing"; addition = replacement of "nothing" by tL items). However, such a view would be unnecessarily cumbersome and unproductive. This miscue category has been sub-divided to reflect several types of substitution miscues that occur in the data.

Expansive substitutions are tL lexical items that expand or extend the semantic range of the sL message. Most often the semantic range of the sL message is a partially subsumed or inferred category in the semantic range of the tL items. This sub-category will be limited to those instances in which there exist tL lexical items that could more exactly reflect the sL message but which, for some reason, have not been used in the interpretation; e.g.:

sL: "... *If I was studying French history...* "

                    <u>nod</u>
tL: ... IDEA ME STUDYwg ABOUT FRANCE POSS CULTURE ...

Back translation of tL: '[An] idea I study about France, its culture...'

The lexical item CULTURE has used as a replacement of the meaning of the sL lexical lexical item *history*. In this case there clearly exists an exact tL equivalent for the sL lexical item *history*. For some reason, however, the interpreter chose not to use the equivalent lexical item. Of course, one could argue that a study of the culture of a people could include a study of the history of that people. However, a study of the culture of a people necessarily implies more than a study of their history, while a study of the history of a people does not necessarily imply a study of the culture of that people. Thus, the interpreter has overextended the meaning of the sL message.

Restrictive substitutions are tL lexical items that restrict or constrict the semantic range of the sL message. Most often the semantic range of the interpretation is a partially subsumed or inferred category in the semantic range of the sL message. This subcategory is also restricted to instances in which there are lexical items that more exactly reflect the sL message; e.g.:

> **sL:** "*... then we started refining that...*"
>
>   _t
>
> **tL:**   ... ME, START CHANGE++ R-E-F-I-N-E ...
>
> **Back translation of tL:** 'Me? I started changing, refine ...'

The substitution in the interpretation is the tL singular ME for the sL plural *we*. In this instance the sL message makes it clear that the work of refining was a group effort. Preceeding context makes it clear that the group consisted of linguists, test designers, and interpreters. The interpretation, however, conveys the meaning that the work of refining was solely the responsibility of the speaker. Thus, the tL substitution has restricted the semantic range of the sL message.

Cohesive substitutions are tL lexical items that alter the grammatical cohesive relations intended or established by the sL text. This sub-category is restricted to those instances in which a more exact corollary for reflecting the desired sL cohesion exists in the tL; e.g.

sL: *"... More importantly I have to decide..."*

    (brow raise)   _____<u>nodding</u>
tL: ... (2h) ALSO   ME MYSELF-inc MUST DECIDE..."

Back translation of tL: 'Also I myse -- must decide... '

In this instancve the tL ALSO has been substituted for the sL cohesive *more importantly.* In this instance the speaker has used "more importantly" to establish a comparison to make the preceeding utterance, as judged by the speaker, less crucial than what follows. The tL ALSO, however, is a simple additive conjunction which does not convey the fact that what follows is judged by the speaker to be more important. Thus the tL substitution conveys a different type of grammatical cohesion.

Unrelated Substitutions are tL lexical items that totally deviate from the sL message and have no immediate sL motivation. While such substitutions do add new information to the tL message (and hence might be considered lexical additions), they can properly be considered substitutions since the tL items used replace expected tL items; e.g.:

sL: *"...but the U.S.* [job] *market necessitates urgently needs interpreters* [skilled] *in two languages..."*

    (body shift rt)   (brow raise _____<u>nod</u>)) (body back
tL: TRANSFER-rt WORK FOR C-O-M-M-O-N-M-A-R-K-E-T THAT-rt <u>PLACE</u>

)   _____<u>nod</u>
INDEX-arc PEOPLE MUST* SKILL* TWO LANGUAGE+ INTERPRET ...

Back translation of tL: '... transfer to ? work for [the] common market that place [of transfer] those people definitely must be very skilled interpreting two languages...

In this instance, clearly the tL substitution of the fingerspelled item C-O-M-M-O-N-M-A-R-K-E-T is unrelated to the sL message *U.S.* [job] *market*. Furthermore, nowhere in the preceeding text is there any information that could be construed as motivating this substitution; there is no mention of the European job market or the European Common Market. While it is true that the interpretation expands the semantic range of the sL message (and thus might be considered an expansive substitute), the fact that there is no relation between the two determines inclusion in this subcategory. Unlike expansive or restrictive substitutions, in which a tL substitution can be respectively considered a superordinate or subordinate category of the sL item, there is here no relation between the tL substitution and the sL item. This is also borne out by the fact that the interpreter chose to fingerspell common market, which in this case, confers proper noun status. While the sL message was directed at the employment situation for interpreters in America ("*U.S.* [job] *market*"), the interpretation can only be understood to refer to the employment situation for interpreters in those European countries who are members of the European Economic Community which is popularly referred to as the Common Market. Thus, the tL substitution neither expands or restricts the semantic range of the sL message—it totally deviates from the sL message.

Intrusions

This category of miscues refers to instances in which the structure of the tL is abandoned or ignored and the structure of the sL is adhered to in the interpretation. The result is that the interpreter has not *interpreted* the sL message but rather produced a full or partial transliteration. Consequently, the tL message consists of utterances that are ungrammatical and unacceptable in the tL. Additionally, for those consumers who are dependent upon the interpreter, the tL message may be only marginally intelligible and decipherable (depending on their degree of competence in the sL).

Even minor intrusions increase the likelihood that the tL message will be only partially understood or misunderstood.

Lexical Instrusions refer to the "literal" rendering of certain lexical items within an otherwise generally acceptable tL utterance. The result is that the tL message consists of a partial transliteration. Often such partial transliterations make it difficult or impossible to receive accurately the tL message, e.g.:

> sL: "….*we* [spoken language and sign language interpreters] *testify with one voice…*"

> tL: "…US-TWO If-FIT-IN-rt ONE V̲OICE…"

> **Back translation of tL:** ". . .the two of us merge together [using? with?] a sinlge vocal apparatus."

The intrusion is the sign V̲OICE. In this example, the sL *one voice* is used metaphorically and does not refer to the vibrations of the vocal folds to produce sounds. The tL V̲OICE, on the other hand, is not used metaphorically in the tL, and so its use conveys quite a different meaning from that intended by the sL message. In fact, given the unpleasant and unsuccessful experiences of many Deaf people with speech training and their attitudes toward oralism, it is possible that the interpretation conveys an opposite to the positive and cooperative tone of the sL message.

Certainly lexical intrusions could be viewed as a separate subcategory of substitution miscues (i.e. "literal" substitutions). However, since, in these instances, it is clear that the interpreter deals only with the form of lexical items in the sL message, and not with meaning, it seems more appropriate to consider them intrusions and be able to account for the influence that the sL message form has on the formulation of the tL message. Perhaps miscues of this type would be more accurately called "glossing" intrustions, since the intrusion most often consists of treating a sL lexical item as a gloss for a tL sign and then producing that sign without regard for context or semantics.

Syntactic Intrusions result from the (almost) total and inappropriate adherence to the syntax of the sL in the production of the tL message, resulting in an inappropriate and unacceptable tL utterance. This subcategory will, of course, not include those instances in which the syntactic structures of the tL message and sL message are similar, since the tL utterance would be appropriate and acceptable; e.g.:

> **sL:** "*...so you have an idea what I'm trying to ah get at...*"
>
> <u>   nodding</u>
> **sL:** "...S-O YOU GET IDEA O-F (1h)"WHAT" MINE GOAL "WELL"...
>
> **Back translation of tL:** "...so you obtain idea of what my objective is umm..."

The speaker is saying that the audience understands what the speaker is getting at; the interpreter has, for a moment, not taken in the meaning of the sL message, which would best be conveyed by use of the tL item UNDERSTAND . It is interesting to note that sL *have* was replaced by tL GET. The interpreter seems to have used the tL lexical items S-O YOU GET IDEA O-F to replace the sL phrase *so you have an idea of.* Further support that this was the case comes from the interpreter's insertion of fingerspelled O-F in the tL utterance.

Anomalies

This category of miscues refers to instances in which the tL message is meaningless or confused and cannot be reasonably accounted for or explained by another miscue type. Often anomalous tL utterances arise because the interpreter has misheard or misunderstood a portion of the sL message or because the interpreter has incorrectly merged discrete units of sL information.

tL Utterance Anomalies are tL utterances that are meaningless. Such miscues may arise, for example, from the absence of clearly indicated nonmanual signals required by the tL syntax, or because the tL message is conveyed telegraphically (thus requiring the use of cloze skills[1] to determine the meaning of the tL message). Miscues of this type may also reflect misunderstanding of the sL message; e.g.:

> **sL:** *"The matiere courses were taken in the other departments..."*

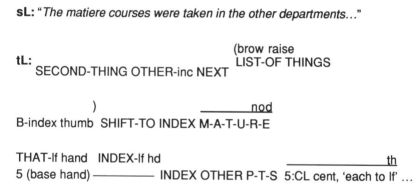

> **Back translation of tL:** ' second item of the next list of items first item
> second item mature that that there other p-t-s each careless p-t-s...'

There are three main reasons why the tL utterance is meaningless. First, the interpreter has apparently misheard the sL item *matiere* and has produced a tL item that not only is unrelated to the sL item but also drastically alters the meaning. Bounded by pauses, the tL utterance presumably expresses a complete message in the tL. However, the lack of a verb renders understanding of the tL utterance difficult if not impossible. Third, the referent for the initial use of the left hand (5) is not provided, nor does previous context provide such a referent. The second use of the left hand (5:CL) is equally unintelligible since the apparent referent (OTHER P-T-S) is presumably an inexact rendering of OTHER D-E-P-T-S. If the tL utterance contained only one of these miscues, it is possible that knowledge of the subject matter and highly developed cloze skills would enable a Deaf person to understand the utterance (although it is difficult to imagine that even the most knowledgeable and skillful person could deduce *matiere* from fingerspelled M-A-T-U-R-E.

tL Interpretation Anomalies   are instances in which the interpretation either contains a tL utterance for which there is no sL message motivation or omits significant portions of the sL message. While miscues of this type do involve the addition or omission of information to the sL message, the extent of the information added or omitted is such that it is inappropriate to consider them instances of lexical addition or lexical omission. What is of significance in this category is the sheer quantity of information that is added or omitted without appropriate sL message motivation; e.g.:

sL: "...*looking at curriculum designed in such ways means that I'm going to address also six content considerations...*"

<u>nod</u>
tL: "...THAT MY FEEL ABOUT LIST-OF

                    "WAIT-A-MIN "

<u>nod</u>	<u>nodding</u>	<u>cond</u>
IF WE FOLLOW THAT IDEA+	IDEA-EXPAND FOR LIST-OF,	
(A-hand hold)—		INDEX-ctr

                                      (head down   )
WE MUST-inc "WELL" "WELL" MUST FOCUS-ON ctr/rt SIX (2h)IDEA-alt

THINK ABOUT WHAT WILL INCLUDE IN* THAT LIST-OF

  (body shift rt   )
ME WANT ME EXPALIN ABOUT THAT SIX LIST OF ...

Back translation of tL: '...that (is) my feeling about (the) list of items wait now if we follow these ideas (and) expanded idea for (the) list of items there we must well must focus on ? six ideas think about what will (be) included in that list of items I want I explain about that six list of items...'

Assume, for the sake of discussion, that the medial portion of the tL utterance (...IF WE...IN* THAT LIST-OF) is a marginally acceptable rendition of the sL message. Clearly the initial and final portions of the tL utterance present information that is outside the scope of the sL message. Such embellishments cannot be readily accounted for by claiming a case of lexical addition. Nor, since the medial portion of the tL utterance provides a marginally acceptable rendition of the sL message, can these additions be explained by claiming a case of misunderstanding the sL message. Moreover, the preceeding and following sL text contains nothing that could be construed as motivating the interpreter to produce the initial and final portions of the tL message.

Miscue occurrence

Previous sections have provided a taxonomy of interpreter miscues. This section will detail the extent to which each category and subcategory of miscue occurs. In order to calculate the number of miscues without inflating the totals, each miscue taken was assigned to the single most appropriate miscue category. Thus, for example, if a sign occurred in the tL message that added information to the sL message and was also an instance of lexical intrusion, only a single miscue would be recorded. While this procedure may preclude determining the complete and cumulative effect of certain miscues, it avoids inflating the occurrence of miscues by attributing a single miscue to only one category.

The total number of miscues and the distribution of miscues is provided in Table 5.1. In addition, this table also indicates the percentage of total miscues in each category.

Table 5.1. Distribution of Miscues.

	Int. 1	Int. 2	Int. 3	Int. 4	Int. 5	Int. 6
Sample min.	8	4	8	8	4	5
Total miscues	139	42	135	96	65	20
Omissions	31	9	42	37	22	10
%	22.3	21.4	31.1	38.6	33.8	50.0
Additions	27	15	12	13	12	3
%	19.4	35.7	8.9	13.5	18.5	15.0
Substitutions	17	7	33	20	15	3
%	12.2	16.7	24.4	20.8	23.1	15.0
Intrusions	24	4	22	11	4	1
%	17.3	9.5	16.3	11.5	6.1	5.0
Anomalies	40	7	26	15	12	3
%	28.8	16.7	19.3	15.6	18.5	15.0

While subsequent sections will address each miscue category in some detail, there are some interesting observations that pertain to the total number of miscues. Given that the sampling procedure used to select the interpreter data (Ch. 3) yielded uneven sample sizes, it will be helpful to equalize momentarily the sample sizes and extrapolate total miscues on the basis of adjusted sample size. An upper and lower extrapolated sample size is provided in Table 5.2.

In the previous chapter, Table 4.10. provided the average lag times of the interpreters. It is significant that the two interpreters with the longest lag times (Int. 2 3.0 sec.; Int. 6 4.8 sec.) have the lowest number of recorded miscues while two of the interpreters with the shortest lag times (Int. 3 1.7 sec.; Int. 1 2.4 sec.) have the highest number of recorded miscues. It would appear, then, that there is a definite relationship between lag time and miscues. That is, increased lag time provides the interpreter with the necessary sL information to avoid most miscue types.

Table 5.2. Extrapolated miscues, sample sizes equalized.

	Int. 1	Int. 2	Int. 3	Int. 4	Int. 5	Int. 6
Miscues per min.	17.4	10.5	16.9	12	16.2	4
Total in: 8 mins.	139	84	135	96	130	32
5 mins.	87	52	84	60	81	20
4 mins.	70	42	68	48	65	16

Increased lag time, however, does not, in itself, guarantee diminished possibility of miscues. This is evidenced by Int. 5 who has the third highest average number of miscues per minute (16.2) and also has the third greatest lag time (2.7 sec.). That time lag alone is not the single cause or determinant for miscues can be seen in the performance of Int. 1 and Int. 4. The time lag for each of these interpreters is identical (2.4 sec.), yet Int. 4 has approximately 30% fewer recorded miscues than Int. 1 (96 and 139, respectively). If time lag alone were the cause for miscues, one would expect the number of recorded miscues to be closer than they are. Subsequent sections will continue to address the relation of time lag to miscues as it applies to each miscue category.

It is interesting to note that for those interpreters with hearing parents (Int. 4, Int. 5, and Int. 6) interpretation is from their dominant, first language (English) into their weaker, second language (ASL). (It could convincingly be argued that even for those interpreters with Deaf parents English, and not ASL, is their dominant language since, for example, their academic experiences have all been in English). For spoken language interpreters it is generally recommended that interpretation should be from the weaker, second language into the dominant, native language (Seleskovitch, 1978). This recommendation is based on the assumption that one has greater expressive control of the dominant language and that one's comprehension of the weaker language exceeds expressive skills in the weaker language. If these assumptions are true for Sign Language interpreters, then in ASL-English interpretation one would expect interpreters with hearing parents to exhibit fewer miscues than they do in English-to-ASL interpretation. However, it may be that, given the fundamental importance of comprehension to the interpretation process, the processing of information is more smoothly and accurately accomplished when the original message is delivered in the interpreter's dominant language. Thus, one would expect fewer miscues in English-ASL situations for interpreters for whom English is the dominant language. Certainly this is an area that warrants further investigation.

Omissions

As noted above, omission miscues refer to instances in which sL information does not appear in the tL interpretation. This category refers specifically to lexically conveyed sL information since omissions of sL sentences of major portions of sentences are treated as anomalies. Omissions were sub-divided to reflect omissions of three levels of information—morphological, lexical, and cohesive. Table 5.3 presents the number of omissions per sub-category and the percentage of total lexically-related miscues (i.e. excluding Anomalies and Syntactic Intrusions) represented by each sub-category.

As Table 5.3. indicates, lexical omissions are the most frequent type of omission, followed by cohesive omissions and then morphological omissions. While frequency information is revealing, it does not necessarily mirror the significance of these sub-categories. One way of viewing the significance of these miscue sub-categories is the potential for consumer recovery of each type of omitted information.

Table 5.3. Omission miscues.

	Int. 1	Int. 2	Int. 3	Int. 4	Int. 5	Int. 6
Lexically-related miscues	90	33	105	78	52	17
Morphological Omissions	7	0	1	6	2	1
%	7.7	0	.9	7.7	3.8	5.8
Lexical Omissions	20	4	25	17	12	5
%	22.2	12.1	23.8	21.8.	23.1	29.4
Cohesive Omissions	4	5	16	14	8	4
%	4.4	15.1	15.2	17.9	15.4	23.5
Total Omissions	31	9	42	37	22	10
%	34.3	27.2	39.9	47.4	42.3	58.7

Viewed from this perspective, one could argue that lexical omissions, although most frequent, are less severe than cohesive or morphological omissions. Certainly the possibility that consumers could apply cloze skills[1] (and hence recover omitted information) is greater for lexical omissions than for the other two sub-categories. Additionally, depending on the type of omitted information, the overall meaning of the tL interpretation may be only slightly different from the sL message (e.g. omitting the information value of "very "in "I'm very busy right now"). Of course the suggestion that consumers may be able to recover omitted information or that the omitted information may not be crucial is not meant to diminish the importance of lexical omissions. Clearly there are lexical omissions that are unrecoverable and do result in significant changes to the sL message.

Cohesive and morphological omissions, however, would appear to be more problematic than some types of lexical omission since they are not recoverable and almost always significantly alter the meaning of the sL message. For example, if the cohesive value of a conjunction is omitted (e.g. "however"), then one may have no way of knowing that two statements are being offered as contrasts or that the second is intended to limit or clarify the claims of the first. Additionally, while certain types of lexical omission may result in a totally meaningless tL utterance (which, presumably, can be readily identified by consumers and dealt with accordingly), morphological and cohesive omissions yield tL utterances which are meaningful. However, the consumer has no way of knowing that the tL meaning that has been conveyed is different than the meaning of the sL message. Thus, while the potential for recovery exists with certain types of lexical omission, recovery potential for morphological and cohesive omissions is severely restricted.

An uninformed view of simultaneous interpretation might hold that the shorter the time lag between sL message and tL message the less likelihood there is that the interpreter will omit information. However the data in this study run counter to that popular notion. If we consider the performance of the two interpreters with the longest lag time (Int. 6 and Int. 2), we find that they have the lowest number of omissions per minute (an average of 2.0 and 2.3, respectively). Conversely, two of the interpreters with the shortest lag times (Int. 3 and Int. 4) have the highest number of omissions per minute (5.3 and 4.6, respectively). A plausible explanation is that increased lag time enhances overall comprehension of the sL message and allows the interpreter to determine the informational and functional value of morphological and cohesive units as well as lexical items. Conversely, a compressed lag time places the interpreter in a quasi-shadowing task in which speech articulation and sign production rate differences may result in increased omissions as the interpreter strives to "keep up "with the speaker.

Additions

As noted above, addition miscues refer to instances in which information that has no motivation or corollary in the sL message appears in the tL message; they are specifically, lexically conveyed tL information, since addition of tL sentences or major portions of sentences are treated as anomalies. Additions were divided into three subcategories: nonmanual, lexical, and cohesive. Table 5.4. presents the number of additions per subcategory and the percentage of total lexically-related miscues (i.e. excluding Anomalies and Syntactic Intrusions) represented by each subcategory.

Table 5.4. Addition miscues.

	Int. 1	Int. 2	Int. 3	Int. 4	Int. 5	Int. 6
Total Lexically-related miscues	90	33	105	78	52	17
Non-manual additions	11	8	2	4	9	1
%	12.3	24.2	1.9	5.1	17.3	5.9
Lexical Additions	13	6	7	8	3	1
%	14.4	18.2	6.7	10.3	5.8	5.9
Cohesive Additions	3	1	3	1	0	1
%	3.3	3.0	2.9	1.3	0.0	5.9
Total Additions	27	15	12	13	12	3
%	30.0	45.4	11.4	16.7	23.1	17.7

As with omissions, it will be helpful to view addition miscues from the perspective of the consumer's ability to recover the intended sL meaning from a tL utterance to which information has been added. Certainly if a lexical addition occurs that results in a meaningless tL utterance, consumers are made aware that something is awry. In order to retrieve the sL meaning, however, consumers would have to delete the added tL item. It is unlikely that this would be consumers' first response; it may well be that they will assume that something has been omitted from the tL utterance and attempt to apply cloze abilities, which could compound the miscue. Of course, not all lexical additions significantly alter the meaning of the sL message (e.g., adding the information value of "very" to "I'm busy right now.").

It is worth noting that those interpreters with the shortest lag time exhibit the greatest number of lexical and cohesive additions. As with omissions, this may be partly attributable to the level of comprehension attained by the interpreters before producing the tL message. Those interpreters with shorter lag times are frequently in a position of dealing with the sL message in an almost literal fashion (cf. Intrusion Miscues) and producing tL utterances before totally comprehending the sL message. It is possible that, in an effort to repair a more or less literal rendition of the sL message, these interpreters add lexical and cohesive items. However, since their comprehension of the sL message is more segmented than that of interpreters with longer lag times, lexical and cohesive items are added which are not always in harmony with the sL message.

As noted in above, the subcategory of nonmanual additions has been restricted to a particular subset of nonmanual behaviors (i.e. 'mm', 'cs', 'th', 'puffed cheeks', 'pursed lips', and 'intense'). By far the two most frequently added nonmanual behaviors are are 'th' and 'mm'. In fact, of the total of 35 nonmanual additions, these two account for 68% (14 and 10, respectively). One possible explanation for nonmanual additions is that there may be certain manual signs and nonmanual behaviors that were erroneously acquired, learned, or perceived by the interpreter as bound to manual signs. The interpretation of a sL message that involves one of these signs would automatically, but incorrectly, result in production of the nonmanual behavior assumed to be "required."

Another possible, but certainly less satisfying, explanation for nonmanual additions is that interpreters include such behaviors in order to "look like" they are using the tL. It is possible that the interpreters know that these nonmanual behaviors occur in ASL but do not have a clear understanding of their meaning and produce the tL message without accurately accounting for the semantic values of the nonmanual items in an effort to produce acceptable tL utterances (not unlike trying to affect an accent). If this were a major motivation for nonmanual additions, however, one would expect them to be more frequent than they are. Their relatively limited occurrence would seem to suggest that some other factor motivates these additions—possibly the failure to view them as distinct from the manual signs with which they co-occur.

Substitutions

Miscues in this category replace sL information by information in the tL message at variance with the intent of the source. Substitution miscues have been divided into expansive, restrictive, cohesive, and unrelated. Table 5.5. presents the number of substitutions per subcategory and the percentage of total lexically-related miscues represented by each sub-category.

Substitution miscues, like addition miscues, generally offer the consumer very little possibility of a) recognizing that the tL message is different than the sL message, and b) attempting to recover or retrieve the intended sL meaning. The major reason for this is that the substituted tL item does not result in an ungrammatical tL utterance nor, except in a few cases of unrelated substitutions, in a tL utterance that is semantically marked. Thus, lacking syntactic or semantic signals to the contrary, the consumer can only accept the tL utterance "at face value."

Table 5.5. Substitution miscues.

	Int. 1	Int. 2	Int. 3	Int. 4	Int. 5	Int. 6
Total Lexically-related miscues	90	33	105	78	52	17
Expansive substitutions	6	2	8	7	4	0
%	6.7	6.0	7.6	8.9	7.7	0.0
Restrictive substitutions	4	0	13	4	7	1
%	4.4	0.0	12.4	5.1	13.5	5.8
Cohesive substitutions	1	35	3	6	1	0
%	1.1	9.0	2.8	7.7	1.9	0.0
Unrelated substitutions	6	2	8	3	3	2
%	6.7	6.0	7.6	3.8	5.8	11.8
Total subs.	18.9	21.0	30.4	25.5	28.9	17.6

Clearly, however, not all instances of substitution are equally serious or problematic for the consumer. Expansive and restrictive substitutions, for example, while not rendering the exact equivalent of the meaning of the sL, nevertheless are not totally unrelated to the sL meaning. Of the two, restrictive substitutions would seem to be less problematic, since the tL substitution, although conveying less information than intended, does not add information to or overextend the sL intent. Thus, in terms of intended sL semantic range, restrictive substitutions result in "parts" being conveyed for "wholes." Resultant tL messages are "accurate" as far as they go—they just do not go far enough.

Expansive substitutions are generally more problematic, since they convey more information than intended by the originator of the sL message. Since these miscues convey "wholes" for "parts," a consumer acting on the basis of a tL message containing an expansive substitution might frequently be in error. A consumer acting on the basis of a tL message containing a restrictive substitution, however, would rarely be in error, though not "correct" often enough when compared with the full meaning of the sL message.

Cohesive substitutions are more problematic since they alter the intended relationships established in the sL text. Such substitutions, since they convey a type and level of cohesion different from that intended by the sL message, directly impair the consumer's ability to discern accurately, for example, intended temporal, causal, additive, or adversative relations. Accurately conveying these relations is essential if consumers are to be able to understand appropriately a speaker's particular line of reasoning, value judgments, and opinions, and, in particular, sequences of events.

Unrelated substitutions (and indeed all types of substitutions) pose particular problems for consumers. Since such substitutions appear to make sense, the consumer is likely to accept a tL utterance containing such a substitution at face value. The consumer, of course, is unaware that the resultant tL utterance deviates from the sL message.

It is not surprising that the two interpreters with the longest lag time have the fewest substitution miscues and the interpreter with the shortest lag time has, by far, the greatest number of substitution miscues. This is most probably a direct function of the level of comprehension of the sL message that the interpreter has gained prior to producing the tL utterance. Clearly, the more accurately the interpreter understands the sL message, the more likely it is that the interpreter will be able to convey the intended sL meaning appropriately and accurately.

Intrusions

This category of miscues refers to instances in which the structure of the tL is abandoned and the structure of the sL is adhered to in rendering the tL message. Intrusions have been subdivided into lexical intrusions (the "literal" rendering of sL lexical items) and syntactic intrusions (inappropriate adherence to the syntax of the sL). Table 5.6 presents the number of lexical intrusions and the percentage of total lexically-related miscues represented by lexical intrusions. Table 5.6 also presents the number of syntactic intrusions and the percentage of total syntactically-related miscues (both syntactic intrusions and anomalies) represented by syntactic intrusions.

Table 5.6. Intrusion miscues.

	Int. 1	Int. 2	Int. 3	Int. 4	Int. 5	Int. 6
Total Lexically-related miscues	90	33	105	78	52	17
Lexical Intrusions	15	2	18	8	3	1
%	16.7	6.1	17.1	10.3	5.8	5.9
Syntactically-related miscues	49	9	30	18	13	3
%	18.4	22.2	13.3	16.6	7.7	0.0
Total Intrusions	24	4	22	11	4	1
% of all miscues	17.3	9.5	16.3	11.5	6.1	6.0

There is a sense in which lexically-related intrusions could be viewed as instances of expansive or restrictive substitutions or, as mentioned above, instances of "literal" substitution. Historically, English word glosses have been used to refer to, to discuss and/or to label signs. However, since the range of meanings of a given sign and of the English word used to gloss that sign are rarely, if ever, congruent, problems arise when individuals, particularly Sign Language teachers and interpreters, fail to realize or remember this. Thus, for example, the ASL sign that means "to go fast by foot" is most often glossed by the English word *run*. The word *run*, however, as used by speakers of English is used to convey many more meanings than "to go fast by foot." Each of these other meanings (e.g. to flow; to stand for office) would be conveyed in ASL by separate and distinct signs. In order to determine which meaning is intended and hence which sign to use to convey that meaning, the interpreter needs to understand exactly the sL message. The degree to which the interpreter understands the sL message is, of course, directly related to lag time.

It is not surprising, then, that as a group the three interpreters with the longest lag times (Int. 6, Int. 2, Int. 5) have an average lexical intrusion rate of 0.48 per minute while the three interpreters with the shortest lag times have an average rate that is three times greater (1.66 per minute). Increased lag time, it appears, reduces the likelihood of lexical intrusions, presumably because the interpreters more accurately comprehend the sL message.

Interestingly, the same ratio (1:3) appears in the case of syntactic intrusions. The three interpreters with the longest lag time have an average syntactic intrusion rate of 0.2 per minute while the other three interpreters have a rate of 0.66 per minute. It is readily apparent that a shorter lag time necessarily constrains the interpreter to the syntactic structures of the sL, while a longer lag time at least makes it more possible for the interpreter to produce syntactically appropriate tL utterances or, at a minimum, more tL-like utterances.

Syntactic intrusions present several problems to consumers, all of which decrease the likelihood that the sL-based tL utterance will be accurately understood. The obvious difficulty is that accurate comprehension of such utterances is directly related to competence in the sL. The very presence of an interpreter, however, is an indication that at least some of the consumers either lack competence in the sL or prefer not to test their competence by dealing directly with the sL. A second problem arises because syntactic intrusions occur intermittently and rather randomly. The result is a type of cognitive and linguistic dissonance for the consumer that can only be resolved if the consumer is capable of and engages in what can be called retrospective code-switching, but consumers thus engaged, may be unable to attend fully to subsequent portions of the tL message. A third problem, which is actually a consequence of syntactic intrusions, has to do with the cumulative effect of syntactic intrusions on the level of confidence that consumers have in the interpreter. If miscues of this type errode the consumer's confidence level, then the interpreter's performance (and competence) continues to be questioned even when no syntactic intrusions or other miscues are evident.

Anomalies

This category of miscues refers to instances in which the tL message is confused or meaningless as well as instances in which the tL message either contains a superfluous tL utterance or omits a significant portion of the sL message. The sub-category "tL utterance anomalies "will be restricted to instances in which the tL message is confused or meaningless and which cannot be readily explained by other miscue types. tL interpretation anomalies will refer to instances of superfluous tL utterances or omission of significant portions of the sL message. Table 5.7 presents each sub-category of miscue and the percentage of total syntactically-related (i.e. syntactic intrusions and anomalies) miscues represented by each sub-category.

It is worth noting, once again, that lag time seems to play a critical role in causing miscues of this type. In the case of tL utterance anomalies, it is not surprising that the two interpreters with the shortest lag times produce more confused and meaningless tL utterances. In fact, the average number of anomalous tL utterances per minute for Int. 3 and Int. 1 is more

Table 5.7. Miscue anomalies.

	Int. 1	Int. 2	Int. 3	Int. 4	Int. 5	Int. 6
Total syntactically-related miscues	49	9	30	18	13	3
tL Utterance Anomalies	25	5	21	10	8	2
%	51.0	55.6	70.0	55.6	61.5	66.7
tL Interpretation Anomalies	15	2	5	5	4	1
%	30.6	22.2	16.7	27.8	30.8	33.3
Total Anomalies	40	7	26	15	12	3
%	81.6	77.8	86.7	83.4	92.3	100.0

than three times the average for Int. 6 and Int. 2 (2.85 and .8 miscues per minute, respectively). It seems inescapable that the more the interpreter is constrained by shortened lag time to mirror the syntactic structures of the sL, the more likely it is that syntactic intrusions and tL utterance anomalies will result.

It is generally true that tL utterance anomalies might be accounted for by applying several of the miscue categories to the tL utterance. Such an exercise, while theoretically intriguing, is neither an efficient nor intuitively satisfying means of addressing such miscues. Additionally, from the perspective of consumer recoverability, such an exercise is not one in which consumers are likely to engage themselves—"first add this, then delete that, then substitute this...." It is more appropriate, for purposes of this study, to avoid such convoluted *post-facto* rationalizations or reconstructions and treat such cases as tL utterance anomalies.

The relationship between tL interpretation anomalies and time lag is an interesting one. A reasonable assumption would be that a longer lag time increases the probability for superfluous tL utterances and for omissions of significant portions of the sL message. Conversely, it might be assumed that a shorter time lag would reduce the probability of both. However, the data presented in this study do not provide support for either assumption. Those interpreters with the shortest lag times (Int. 3, Int. 1, Int. 4) have an average of 8.3 tL interpretation anomalies while the three with the longest lag times have an average of 2.3 tL interpretation anomalies. More interesting, however, is the distribution of these miscues.

Clearly the notion that a shorter lag time reduces the likelihood of significant omissions is not borne out by these data. Even if the performance of Int. 1 (which is quite extreme) is excluded, those interpreters with shorter lag times still exhibit more significant omissions than one would expect given the quasi-shadowing task in which they are engaged.

What is interesting, and perhaps unexpected, is that a shorter lag time does not appear to reduce the likelihood of superfluous additions. Again, even excluding the performance of Int. 1, those interpreters with shorter lag times still exhibit approximately the same number of superfluous additions as those with longer lag times. It is possible that there is a causal relation between superfluous additions and significant omissions. That is, given a shorter

Table 5.8. Distribution of tL interpretation anomalies.

	Int. 1	Int. 2	Int. 3	Int. 4	Int. 5	Int. 6
Total tL interpretation anomalies	15	2	5	5	4	1
Superfluous additions	8	1	2	1	1	0
%	53.3	50.0	40.0	20.0	25.0	0.0
Significant omissions	7	1	3	4	3	1
%	46.7	50.0	60.0	80.0	75.0	100.0

lag time, if one adds superfluous tL utterances the result may be a longer lag time than the interpreter is comfortable with. One

strategy for compensating for the longer lag time required by the
addition may be to omit significant portions of the subsequent sL
message, thus returning to a shorter lag time.

Because both tL utterance and tL interpretation anomalies are
sentence-level, as opposed to lexical-level miscues, it is especially
revealing to compare the number of tL sentences containing one
of these anomaly miscues with the total number of tL sentences
produced. This comparison is provided in Table 5.9.

From a consumer's perspective, it is worthwhile to note that,
for the most part, a significant number of the total tL sentences
produced by interpreters contain syntactically-related miscues.
Not surprisingly, increased time lag seems to reduce the likelihood
that these types of miscues will occur. For those interpreters with
shorter lag times an average of 31.5% of the total number of tL
sentences they produce contain syntactically-related miscues. On
the other hand, 18.5% of the total tL sentences produced by those

Table 5.9. Sentence-level miscues.

	Int. 1	Int. 2	Int. 3	Int. 4	Int. 5	Int. 6
Total tL sentences	103	48	94	94	41	60
Syntactic Intrusions	9	2	4	3	1	0
%	8.7	4.2	4.2	3.2	2.4	0.0
tL Utterance anomalies	25	5	21	10	8	2
%	24.3	10.4	22.3	10.6	19.5	3.3
tL Interpretation anomalies	15	2	5	5	4	1
%	14.6	4.2	5.3	5.3	9.8	1.7
Total syntactically-related miscues	49	9	26	18	13	3
%	47.6	18.8	27.8	19.1	31.7	5.0

with longer lag times contain syntactically-related miscues. There
are, of course, factors other than time lag that cause syntactically-

related miscues. Int. 5, for example, has the second highest percentage of syntactically-related miscues and yet has the third highest time lag. Int. 4, on the other hand, has the same time lag as Int. 1 (2.4 sec.) and yet has significantly fewer syntactically-related miscues than Int. 1. Increased lag time, then, would seem to be a necessary, but not sufficient, condition to reduce the likelihood of syntactically-related miscues.

Style miscues

The fact that there have been relatively few occasions at which formal ASL has been used has not only resulted in limited exposure to formal ASL for interpreters and Deaf people, but it has also meant that there is virtually no research detailing specific linguistic characteristics that would differentiate formal and informal ASL. Thus it is not possible to make any definitive statements about the extent to which the interpretations and tL utterances in this study reflect a formal register of ASL.

However, there are two sources of subjective information about the formality of the interpreters' performance that are worth reporting here. The first is the reactions of the Deaf consumers who attended the Conference at which these data were collected. The general reactions (and rather heated discussions) following each interpreted session indicated that those consumers felt that the performances of Int.1, Int. 3, and Int. 5 were definitely more informal than those of Int. 2, Int. 4, and Int. 6. Since documentation of the reactions of those consumers was not gathered at that time, a panel of Deaf adults was asked to view the videotape data and comment on the formality/informality of the interpreters performance.

Six Deaf signers (three of whom were native signers) viewed the work copies of the original videotapes. They were asked to indicate whether each interpreter's signing was formal or informal. These ratings confirmed the reactions of the consumers who attended the Conference. Int. 1 and Int. 3 were judged by all to be using more informal than formal ASL. Int. 4 was judged by 3 of the panel (but by only one of the native signers) to be using more formal than informal ASL and Int. 5 was judged to be using more informal ASL by 4 of the panel. Int. 2 and Int. 6 were judged by all to be using more formal than informal ASL.

These intuitive judgments of the panel must be interpreted cautisouly, however. Unlike audiotapes which can be rated without a visual representation of the speaker (e.g. matched guise techniques), ratings of a signer inherently require that the panel of judges see the signer. Thus it is possible that these judgments are influenced by more than the formality/informality of the interpreter's signing (e.g. reputation, prior knowledge, self-fulfilling expectations, general physical appearance of the interpreter).

In order to pursue this issue further, a videotape of a native Deaf signer making a formal conference presentation was examined to determine the frequency of two specific nonmanual, syntactic signals: topic marking and rhetorical questions.

In this admittedly limited sample there was an average of 7 distinct topic signals per minute (range 4-10) and an average of 2.5 rhetorical questions per minute (range 2-4). If these represent a reasonably accurate indication of the occurrence of those two nonmanual syntactic signals in formal ASL, then it is possible to determine the extent to which the performance of the interpreters in this study mirrors these expected occurrence levels.

Table 5.10. Topic signals & rhetorical questions.

	Int. 1	Int. 2	Int. 3	Int. 4	Int. 5	Int. 6	Deaf Signer
Sample size	8 min.	4 min.	8 min.	8 min.	4 min.	5 min.	5 min.
Avg topics/min	1.7	2	3.1	2.1	1	5	7
Avg rhet ?/min	0.3	0.5	0.5	0.6	0.2	1.5	2.5

It should be noted that the figures reported in Table 5.10. reflect the occurrence of unambiguously marked topics and rhetorical questions. There were, for each interpreter, instances of non-manual activity that were possibly attempts at marking topics or rhetorical questions, given their locii of occurrence in the tL utterances; however, the behaviors were ambiguous and could be coded in the transcriptions only as "brow-raise."

While caution is required in the interpretation of these data, it would seem that, in general, the frequency of unambiguous occurrence of these two nonmanual signals in the tL utterances of the interpreters is quite different from that of their occurrence in formal ASL. It is, however, rather surprising that one of the most common devices in ASL for introducing new information and for focusing addressee attention on that information—the rhetorical question—is used so infrequently by the interpreters. It may well be that the occurrence of these signals is depressed by the fact that interpreters control neither content nor content development. Another reason for depressed occurrence might be that other inappropriate (but still syntactically acceptable) tL syntactic strategies are used in lieu of, for example, rhetorical questions. That this, indeed, seems to be the case can be determined by examining the number of interpreter produced wh- and yes-no questions that are inappropriate (i.e. the speaker did not ask a question).

Table 5.11. Wh- & Yes-No questions.

	Int. 1	Int. 2	Int. 3	Int. 4	Int. 5	Int. 6
Avg wh- ?s/min	0.5	0	1.1	0.4	0	0
Avg y/n ?s/min	0.5	0	0.6	0.2	0.2	0

If the performance of Int. 2 and Int. 6 is discounted, the remaining four interpreters average more than twice as many inappropriate wh- and yes-no questions per minute as they do rhetorical questions (0.87 and 0.4, respectively). It is possible then that for these interpreters the frequency of rhetorical questions is depressed because they attempt to accomplish the function of rhetorical questions by producing actual wh- and yes-no questions. While it is not clear to what extent such behavior influences consumer comprehension of the message, one can only speculate that the cumulative effect of such behavior on consumers'affective judgments of speakers can only be negative— after all, who would think positively about someone who asks questions but doesn't wait for the addressee to answer?

Another indication that the tL usage of some of the interpreters reflects a more informal, conversational style is the use of the nonmanual adverb 'th', which conveys the meaning of 'careless' or 'without paying attention.' It has been suggested (Bienvenu, 1984) that the use of this particular nonmanual behavior seems to be restricted to informal, conversational situations. If this is indeed the case, then one would expect no occurrence of this signal (except possibly in cases of direct address or style-shifting) in these tL messages, which are formal lectures. Table 5.12, which excludes such cases, indicates the total occurrences of 'th'and the per minute average. If this signal is restricted to informal use and is therefore an indicator of informal use, it would appear that at least certain portions of the interpreter's performance are more informal than is warranted.

Table 5.12. Occurrence of 'th'signal.

	Int. 1	Int. 2	Int. 3	Int. 4	Int. 5	Int. 6
No. uses of 'th''	11	6	0	2	1	0
Average/minute	1.4	1.5	0	0.2	0.2	0

One possible explanation for the frequent use of this signal is that it may, in the minds of the interpreters, co-occur (or be automatically required) with certain signs. If this is the case, then its occurrence may not indicate a total style shift but rather a learned or acquired lexical limitation.

While the lack of research on formal ASL precludes unambiguous categorization of interpreter performance, there is at least some linguistic evidence (most notably the limited use of rhetorical questions) as well as the subjective ratings of the panel to suggest that, taken as a group, the interpreters'use of the tL is more informal than formal. Further research on formal ASL is certainly needed before this issue can be fully addressed.

Speakers' miscues

That interpreters make miscues is not the most important finding reflected in the data presented here. Interpreters are, after all, human, and it would be unrealistic to expect a total absence of miscues given the cognitive and physical demands with which they must contend. (This is not to say, however, that interpreters should not, and do not, strive for complete accuracy. Nor is this to suggest that interpreters use this reality as a rationalization for complacency.) In addition, a microanalysis of the per-formance of speakers would reveal that they too exhibit linguistic behaviors that would be termed miscues if compared with the linguistic norms of English, for example. Such speaker behaviors might include, among others, false starts, mispronunciations, inappropriate intonation patterns, errors in lexical selection, ungrammatical sentence structures and ambiguous referencing.

Not only do such speaker behaviors appear in the transcripts of informal, casual interactions (e.g. Tannen, 1984), but they also appear in the transcripts of formal interactions as well. Consider the following examples that are taken from the speaker transcripts in this study:

a. *"...ya'know you hear the original and maybe twenty seconds later you hear with your from your own voice."* ('you hear with your'?; 'you hear from your own'?);

b. *"...so that he could or she could know where he stood as in so far as language proficiency was concerned..."* ('as in so far as'?);

c. *"Okay what I want you to do I we're not there's gonna be certain information..."* (false starts);

d. *"...because what is very easy at a given moment and have only three minutes of length can become... "* ('have only'?);

e. *"...and it had uh certain components into it... "*('components into it'?);

f. *"...and the two things that we thought we could see in the performance was the adaptability of the text the other one being... "*('two things...was...'?).

The point of these examples is simply to illustrate that if one compares the linguistic performance of the speakers in this study with the linguistic norms or expectations of English, it is possible to identify deviations from those norms or expectations that could be termed miscues. While it is outside the scope of this study to quantify such miscues, it should be evident that the sL messages that interpreters are presented with do not always conform to the expectations of the sL. Given this, it would be doubly unrealistic to expect that interpreters, who control neither content nor content development, should be less subject to miscues than speakers who do control content and content development. Thus, it is not surprising that miscues occur in the process of interpretation.

The significance of interpreter miscues

What is a significant finding from the data presented in this chapter is the frequency and distribution of miscues. It must be remembered that the criteria used to identify and tabulate miscues were conservative criteria. Thus, the data reported in this chapter should be viewed as minimum base line data. More liberal criteria for identifying miscues would, of course, increase their frequency and alter the calculations.

Focusing for the moment only on syntactically-related miscues, it is worth noting that only 4.3% of the total tL sentences are clear cases of syntactic intrusion. Thus, it is apparent that, as a group, the interpreters are at least attempting to use the tL (ASL) and are not, as sometimes happens, simply replacing sL lexical items with tL lexical items. That is, the interpreters are trying to interpret not transliterate.

The data on syntactic intrusions, coupled with tL utterance anomalies, provide an indication of how well or accurately the interpreters were able to execute the tL, since lexically-related miscues do not inherently result in unacceptable tL utterances (although they do result in deviations from the intended sL message). Viewed thus, there is quite a range in the performance of the interpreters. Int. 6 achieves the highest rate of generally acceptable tL utterances (95.0%) while Int. 1 has the lowest rate (52.4%). The average of the remaining four interpreters is 75.6% (cf. Table 5.13).

One very likely explanation for this could be the limited exposure of interpreters to ASL used in formal situations. This is because, quite simply, there are still relatively few formal occasions (e.g. conferences, seminars, meetings) at which Deaf people are asked to make presentations and do so in formal ASL. Thus, it is limited opportunity, not limited desire, that results in limited exposure to formal ASL. It should be noted that this limited exposure to formal ASL affects not only interpreters but Deaf people as well (Bienvenu, 1984). Faced with formal sL input for which interpreters have little or no tL analogs, there are three possible outcomes in terms of interpreter performance. The interpreter may produce acceptable tL utterances that reflect an informal, conversational style level in the tL rather than a formal one. A second possibility is that the interpreter may resort to extended lexical replacement (i.e. transliteration) thus mirroring the syntactic structures of the sL. The final possibility is that the interpreter may produce tL utterances that, for a variety of specific linguistic reasons, not only do not convey the sL message but are meaningless or confused tL utterances.

The lack of research detailing characteristics of formal ASL makes it difficult to determine clearly whether interpreter performance reflects informal or formal expectations. However, the ratings of the panel, the relatively infrequent occurrence of rhetorical questions and the use of actual questions by four of the interpreters would seem to indicate that perhaps their performance is more informal than formal. The extent to which interpreters resort to extended lexical replacement, as indicated by syntactic intrusions, is rather minimal. As noted above, only about 4% of the total tL sentences are clear cases of syntactic intrusion. That this figure is so low is undoubtedly a function of the situation in which these data were collected (cf. Ch. 3). In situations where interpreter expectations are not as clearly evident, it is quite likely that instances of intermittent trans-literation would be much more frequent.

The number of tL utterances that are meaningless or confused (i.e. tL utterance anomalies) is greater than one might expect. Approximately 16% of the total tL sentences fall into this category. It is probable that this figure is influenced by the interpreters' perception that transliteration would not be a viable alternative to use in this situation. The constraints of the situation (cf. Ch. 3) are such that a performance behavior (transliteration) that might be used by interpreters to "compensate" for lack of exposure to formal ASL seems to have been suppressed, while a performance behavior that interpreters clearly would want to avoid (i.e. meaningless or confused tL utterances) seems to be inflated. The net result, whatever the influencing causes, is that 20% of the tL sentences are syntactically inappropriate. The degree to which this affects overall consumer comprehension is unknown but clearly those meaningless or confused tL sentences would present a formidable obstacle to consumer recovery of intended sL meaning.

Syntactically-related miscues are not the only obstacle to consumer recovery of intended sL meaning, although they are probably the most severe type of obstacle with which consumers must contend. Lexically-related miscues are also problematic for consumers. Certainly if consumers were aware that a miscue had occurred and if they were aware of the type of miscue, then recovery of the sL meaning might be possible. Given that consumers are almost certainly not aware of the occurrence and type of miscues, it is unlikely that intended sL meanings can be consistently or accurately recovered. It is also not the case that there are only an isolated number of lexically-related miscues with which consumers have to contend (even if they were aware of them).

Table 5.13 provides an indication of the extent and pervasiveness of lexically-related miscues and their relation to the recoverabilty of sL meaning. If lexical miscues are evenly distributed over all tL sentences, then there is slightly less than one such miscue per sentence (an average of .84 per tL sentence). However, lexically-related miscues are not evenly distributed over all tL sentences. In order to more accurately determine their impact, it is necessary to distribute them only over syntactically acceptable tL sentences. This is consistent with the manner of calculating miscues described above. Distributed in this manner, there is slightly more than one miscue per syntactically acceptable tL sentence (an average of 1.21).

Of course not every syntactically acceptable tL sentence contains a lexically-related miscue. Also, not all types of lexically-related miscues are equally serious nor equally problematic for consumers. However the distribution averages that were presented above (.84 and 1.21) cast a slightly different light on the issue of the consumer's ability to recover intended sL meaning. With an average of one lexically-related miscue per sentence, consumers would be constantly presented with tL utterances that differ from or deviate from the intended meaning of the sL utterances. The ability to recover from most types of lexicaly-related miscues would seem to depend upon consumer awareness that a miscue has occurred and on accurately acquired contextual information. Except in very few cases, consumers are, by definition, not likely to to be aware of occurrences of miscues. Even if they were, the ability to recover from a given miscue would seem, in large part, to be predicated upon having accurately recovered from pre-ceding miscues. Assuming, for the moment, that consumers were aware of occurrences of miscues, the mental effort expended in attempting to recover the intended sL meaning would, at best, deflect attention from the content of the sL message and, at worst, might so preoccupy consumers that subsequent portions of the sL message could not be attended to.

Table 5.13. Extent of lexical miscues.

	Int. 1	Int. 2	Int. 3	Int. 4	Int. 5	Int. 6
Total tL sentences	103	48	94	94	41	60
Total syntactically-related miscues	49	9	26	18	13	3
Syntactically acceptable tL serntences	54	39	68	76	28	57
%	52.4	81.1	72.3	80.8	68.3	95.0
Lexically related miscues	90	33	109	78	52	17
Average lexically related miscues per sentence	1.66	0.85	1.60	1.02	1.86	.29

The preceding discussion, of course, treats all lexically-related miscues as if they were equally serious. Since this is clearly not the case, the above discussion rather exaggerates the impact of lexically-related miscues. A clearer indication of their impact can be gained by considering the frequency and distribution of only those miscues that are inherently non-recoverable. Thus, for example, while certain lexical omissions might be recoverable from context, additions or unrelated substitutions are less likely to be recovered by consumers, since there is generally no indication that they have occurred (i.e. consumers are unlikely to suspect or notice the miscue since the resultant tL utterance may be inherently meaningful). Table 5.14 presents the various types of such unrecoverable miscues and their distribution across tL sentences.

The data presented in Table 5.14 make it clear that the need to recover intended sL meaning from "serious " lexical miscues, while still a formidable task, arises in approximately half of the total tL sentences and of the acceptable tL sentences (an average of .40 and .57, respectively). Of course the cumulative effects of not recovering intended sL meanings or of the cognitive energy expended in the process of recovering intended sL meaning are

Table 5.14. Extent of "serious"non-recoverable lexical miscues.

	Int. 1	Int. 2	Int. 3	Int. 4	Int. 5	Int. 6
Morphological omissions	7	0	1	6	2	1
Cohesive omissions	4	5	16	14	8	4
Additions	27	15	12	13	12	3
Unrelated substitutions	6	2	8	3	3	2
Total "serious" lexical miscues	44	22	36	36	25	10
Average miscues per sent. (all tL sentence)	0.43	0.46	0.38	0.38	0.61	0.16
Avg. miscues per acceptable tL sentence	0.81	0.56	0.53	0.47	0.89	0.17

not known. While further research in this area is clearly needed, it would seem likely that full and accurate comprehension of the intended sL meaning is contingent upon active cognitive involvement of those consumers dependent upon interpreters (at least more so than those consumers who have direct access to the sL message).

One factor that seems to be directly related to the overall frequency of miscues is interpreter time lag. While this has been discussed above, it is appropriate at this point to summarize the apparent relationship between time lag and miscues. As will become evident in the next chapter, the major reason why miscues occur seems to be that interpreters do not fully understand the sL message (assuming, of course, a felicity condition i.e. interpreters do not intentionally wish to distort the sL message). Given this, one would expect relatively few (since perfection is a goal to be striven for, but rarely, if ever, attained) miscues from those interpreters who do, in fact, understand the sL message. Comprehension of the sL message necessitates, at a minimum, sufficient linguistic competence in the sL and an adequate quantity of textual material in order to accurately determine, among other things, the meanings of lexical items and the significance of syntactic structures and cohesive devices. Given the constraints of simultaneous interpretation, the quantity of textual material available to the interpreter is directly dependent upon and is a function of the interpreter's ability to maintain a sufficient temporal lag between the production of the sL message and the production of the interpretation of that message. While it is difficult and perhaps impossible to quantify the meaning of "sufficient temporal lag," it seems clear from the data presented in this chapter that the greater the degree of synchrony between production of a sL message and its interpretation, the greater the likelihood of miscues. Other factors being equal, the evidence is consistent with the notion that increased synchrony inherently precludes the interpreter from gaining access to that quantity of textual material necessary for comprehension of the sL message.

That a greater degree of synchrony seems to increase the likelihood of miscues and, conversely, a lesser degree of synchrony seems to reduce the likelihood of miscues has been shown above (e.g. Table 5.2). Perhaps the most convincing evidence of this can be seen in the data on sentence level miscues (Table 5.9). Those interpreters with the shortest time lag produce the highest numbers of syntactically-related miscues while those interpreters with the longest lag time produce the lowest numbers of these miscues. What is more revealing than the actual number of syntactically-related miscues is the percentage of total tL sentences that contain such miscues. In the case of the two interpreters with the shortest lag times an average of 37.7% of all tL sentences contain syntactically-related miscues while for the two interpreters with the longest lag time the average is 11.9%. This would seem to be a clear indication that greater time lag is a necessary, but not sufficient, condition in avoiding syntactically-related miscues.

A final point discussed above concerns the extent to which the interpreter's performance reflects informal, conversational ASL or formal ASL. While the lack of research on formal ASL precludes resolution of this issue, there do seem to be indications that perhaps their performance is more informal and conversational than it is formal. The intuitive judgments of the panel of native and non-native Deaf signers indicate that only Int. 2 and Int. 6 were clearly felt to be using more formal than informal ASL. Int. 1 and Int. 3 were clearly felt by the panel to be using more informal than formal ASL. The majority of the panel felt that Int. 5 was using more informal then formal ASL, and the panel was evenly split in its judgment of Int. 4. In addition to the intuitive judgments of the panel, the relatively limited number of clearly marked topics, the infrequent use of rhetorical questions and the inappropriate occurrence of wh- and yes-no questions all suggest linguistic behaviors that may be quite different than one would expect in formal ASL. An issue raised by this finding is what effect the use of overt conversational behaviors (e.g. asking wh- and yes-no questions) in an obviously non-reciprocal situation has on consumer comprehension and comfort. It is possible that the resulting stylistic dissonance creates an additional cognitive obstacle for consumers. Systematic research in this area, coupled with research on consumer comprehension in general, would be needed to determine the overall effects of interpreter miscues and the effects of specific categories and sub-categories of miscues.

Summary, Chapter 5

Those instances in which the information value of an interpreted text token deviates from the information value of an original text token have been termed miscues. A general taxonomy of miscue types is proposed and defined in this chapter. The general miscue categories are omissions, additions, substitutions, intrusions, and anomalies. These general categories are further sub-divided to provide a greater level of miscue detail.

For each Interpreter the total occurance of miscue tokens in the data sample for the general miscue categories was presented. In every instance a greater number of miscues was identified for interpreters with a shorter lag. Thus, the data suggest a direct correlation between lag time and miscue ocurrance, specifically an inverse correlation (the shorter the lag time, the greater the number of miscues).

Additionally, there appears to be a relationship between lag time and the extent to which an interpreter's tL production matches syntactic production of a native tL Deaf signer delivering a lecture in ASL. Those interpreters with a longer lag time more closely approximated the average occurrence of non-manual topic marking and rhetorical questions. Those interpreters with shorted lag time not only were further from the native ASL production, but also exhibited instances of semantically and syntactically ambiguous tL performance.

In short, this chapter has provided evidence that increased lag time seems to be a necessary, but not sufficient, condition for accurate interpretations to be rendered.

Note Chapter 5

[1] The term Cloze was derived by Taylor (1953) from the concept of closure as used in Gestalt psychology. Gestaltists believe that learning follows a sequence by which one first understands the whole and then proceeds to individual details.

In this context cloze skills are defined as the cognitive ability to supply missing or (partially) distorted information in a linguistic message. The addressee (or in this case the consumer) relies upon knowledge of the syntax and semantics of the language of the message, of the subject matter, and of the speaker to eliminate classes of lexical items that would not or could not be acceptable and then to predict the most likely lexical "filler" for the missing item(s) in the message. For example, suppose that the eighth item in the following English sentence has been distorted: *I had a hard day at the _____ today*. The syntactically acceptable "filler" must be a noun or noun phrase. The addressee's competence in the language and knowledge of the speaker would enable specification of the lexical item "office." Thus, the addressee has been able to narrow the possibilities and, from among those possibilities, complete the distorted message by applying cloze skills.

CHAPTER SIX

PROBABLE MISCUE CAUSES

The taxonomy of miscue types and information about the frequency of each type may be useful in assessing an interpreter's performance or in evaluating the quality of a given interpretation, but its utility in the education and preparation of would-be interpreters and in designing curricula for such purposes seems rather limited. Of much more value in these areas is an indication of probable causes of miscues. If probable miscue causes can be identified, then it will be possible to design curriculum in such a way that the focus is, in part, on developing those skills necessary to minimize the occurrence of miscues. There are certain difficulties in determining the range of possible miscue causes and then discovering a specific cause for a given miscue. Perhaps the major difficulty is that, since interpretation is a cognitive process, only the results of that process are observable. Thus, while it is possible to observe and analyze the behaviors that occur as a result of the process, it is not possible to observe the process itself. This means that although accurate and acceptable tL utterances and miscues can be identified, the processes by which an interpreter produced them can only be indirectly suggested on the basis of directly observable performance.

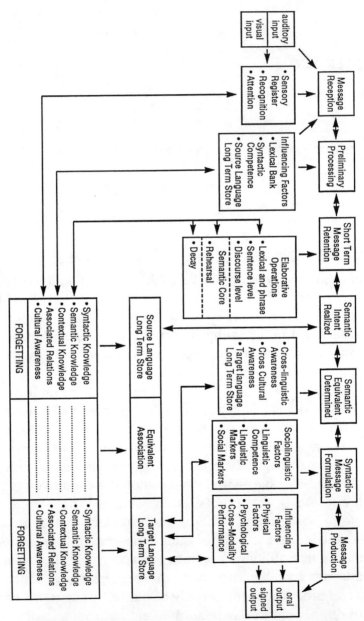

Figure 6.1. Sociolinguistically-sensitive process model

Another difficulty is the fact that interpretation, like other cognitive processes, is minimally a serial process. Actually it is probably more accurately described as serialized parallel processes, because there are undoubtedly several processes functioning simultaneously in an ordered, dependent relationship to each other. Since the process is, in part, serialized (i.e. certain cognitive activities are prerequisites for and prior to other cognitive activities), difficulties encountered in initial stages of the process will affect all subsequent stages of the process. This means that in determining why a given miscue occurred it will be necessary to determine the most likely stage (and the most initial stage) in the sequence of stages at which the miscue could have occurred.

Despite these difficulties, there are miscues whose cause is quite evident. While it may not be possible to determine the cause of all miscues reported in this study with equal confidence, what is necessary is that each of the hypothesized major stages in the interpretation process be validated by identifying miscues that clearly result from a failure to execute accurately the cognitive operations required by that stage in the process. Clearly there will be miscues for which a single cause cannot be unambiguously determined. However, such cases do not negate the existence of process stages. They merely reflect the difficulties of describing and verifying any cognitive process—all such attempts are, of necessity, based on indirect, retrospective data.

The model of the interpretation process presented in Figure 6.1 on the preceding page posits seven major stages: (1) message reception, (2) preliminary processing, (3) short term message retention, (4) semantic intent realization, (5) semantic equivalence determination, (6) syntactic message formulation, and (7) message production. While the hypothesized model also indicates some of the subprocesses and factors that influence these major stages, analysis and validation of these subprocesses is beyond the scope of this study. Additionally, it is not clear that the procedure used to validate the major stages in the process would be the appropriate one to use in validating sub-processes.

Message Reception. It is obvious that before a sL message can be interpreted it must be accurately perceived by the interpreter. Failure to do so will necessarily result in a miscue since, even if subsequent stages in the process are accurately executed, the sL information entering the process is erroneous. Although either visual perception/reception (ASL) or auditory perception/reception (English) can be the source of information input for Sign Language interpreters, the data on which this study are based necessarily involve only the auditory perception/reception of acoustic signals.

Preliminary Processing. Psycholinguistic studies of human information processing (e.g. Broadbent, 1970; Massaro, 1975a & 1975b) indicate that there is a primary recognition process through which the incoming acoustic (and presumably visual) signals pass. It is at this stage, for example, that the phonological rules of the sL are applied to the incoming stimuli and non-phonologically meaningful signals are discarded. It is also at this stage of preliminary processing that incoming sL lexical units are identified, often requiring application of prior syntactic and semantic context. For example, Treisman (1964) suggests a modification of an earlier filter theory in which incoming stimulus items are subjected to successive levels of analysis and the level of analysis reached by a particular stimulus depends both on the physical characteristics of the stimulus and on current biases and expectations.

Short Term Message Retention. Given the linear nature of the incoming sL message, it is necessary that any given element in the string of elements that comprise this message (i.e. lexical items) be temporarily retained until sufficient syntactic and semantic information has been received to properly understand the meaning and/or function of that item. The result is that incoming sL information is analyzed and "chunked" (Goldman-Eisler, 1972) into more abstract units that, ideally, retain the essentials of meaning conveyed by smaller units in the incoming message. These "chunks" are, in turn, analyzed and temporarily retained until some level of understanding of their meaning and/or function has been reached or until they are subsumed by larger "chunks." That is, these "chunks" are analyzable at different levels lexical, phrase, sentence and discourse (Craig and Lockhart, 1972). Accurately understanding a given "chunk" is directly related to the level at which it is analyzed and processed.

Semantic Intent Realized. Having analyzed and "chunked" incoming sL information, the interpreter arrives at some level of comprehension of that portion of the sL message. Ideally, of course, the semantic intent realized by the interpreter is that originally intended by the speaker. Whether it is or not, however, is dependent upon the level at which that portion of the sL message has been analyzed. There are, of course, a number of other factors that influence the extent to which the "chunked" and processed information is understood (e.g. contextual knowledge).

Semantic Equivalence Determined. Once the interpreter has attributed some level of meaning to the sL message (or a portion of the message), it is necessary to determine whether there are linguistic and/or cultural considerations in the tL that might be required to accurately convey that meaning. This stage has also been referred to as transfer of the sL message (Nida and Taber, 1974,). Note that at this point it is the sL meaning, not the sL form, for which the interpreter must determine tL equivalence. Of course, the extent to which the interpreter can do this is directly related to linguistic and cultural competence in the tL.

Syntactic Message Formulation. The interpreter, having ascribed some meaning to the sL message and having determined the tL equivalent of that meaning, must now formulate the tL message that will express that meaning according to the linguistic and cultural norms of the tL. The interpreter's ability to do this is, of course, directly determined by the interpreter's

tL competence. An obvious concern at this point is that the tL
syntactic structure and lexical items that are chosen do not
distort the meaning of the message.

Message Production. The final stage in the process is the actual
production of the tL message. Although for Sign Language
interpreters the tL output can be either gesturally or orally
produced, the data on which this study are based necessarily
involve only gesturally produced tL messages. It is worth
noting that for Sign Language interpreters the communication
modality of the sL message is different than that of the tL
message produced. The fact that there is a modality transfer,
in addition to a meaning transfer, is unique to interpreters
working between signed and spoken languages. For
interpreters working only with signed languages (e.g.
American Sign Language-British Sign Language) or only with
spoken languages (e.g. English-French), no such modality
transfer is needed.

Although the preceding discussion may give the reader the
impression that these major stages are discrete and non-
overlapping, such is not the case. It is likely, for example, that
during the preliminary processing stage, semantic equivalence
issues are being identified and possibly addressed. In fact,
although the model presented in Figure 6.1 and the discussion
above may convey an impression of interpretation as a linear
process, it is probably more accurate and helpful to think of the
process as one in which there is multiple nesting of stages. Such a
view might well better account for the feedback effects of later
stages of the process on earlier stages.

Another factor worth noting at this point is that, for
simultaneous interpretation at least, at any point when the s/t
condition obtains (Ch. 4) the tL utterance being produced by the
interpreter is textually antecedent to the sL utterance being
produced by the speaker at that time. This means that, at a

minimum, the interpreter is producing a tL utterance while receiving and analyzing a different sL utterance. The static nature of the graphic representation of the model and the stage-by-stage discussion of the process above cannot accurately reflect the nature of the interpretation process.

Each of these seven major stages in detail is taken up below, with examples of miscues resulting from failure to execute accurately or appropriately each of these stages. One of the difficulties, however, is that miscues attributed to deficiencies in later stages of the process may actually have arisen because of difficulties in earlier stages; e.g. a failure to determine semantic equivalence may have occurred because of inaccurate or insufficient preliminary processing. Consequently, identification and quantification of miscues as a function of a particular stage in the process cannot always occur with a level of confidence that would yield reliable results and thus it is not reported. In addition, at least for purposes of this study, it is not clear what purpose an exact attribution of miscue causes would serve. Given that the scope of this study is limited to providing evidence for the existence of the major stages of the process, it will be sufficient to present, for each hypothesized stage, a number of miscues that reflect failure to execute that stage accurately.

Message reception

As was noted above, in this study message reception is restricted to the interpreter's auditory perception/reception of an orally produced sL message. The expectation, of course, is that acoustic signals produced by the speaker will be accurately received by the interpreter. When the interpreter's perception of a given set of acoustic signals differs from the signals actually produced by the speaker, the inevitable result is that the subsequent tL message produced by the interpreter differs from the sL message produced by the speaker; e.g.:

sL: "...*The course is offered in English only...*"

	(headshake)	(nod)
tL: "...OUR COURSE++ OFFER		OUR COURSE*

(nod)	rhet-q	tl
OFFER USE LANGUAGE	WHICH	ENGLISH++..."

Back translation of tL: ' ...Our courses offer no, no our course, yes, offer use which language? English...'

Here the interpreter initially perceived the sL message as "...The courses offered..." and appropriately conveyed the misperceived plural, OUR COURSE++ That this is the result of a misperception of the sL message is shown by the interpreter's utterance: the head shake serves to indicate that what was just signed is not correct. The stressed or emphatically produced sign COURSE* not only serves to direct the consumer's attention to the error (COURSE++) but also provides the appropriate information. The head nod that occurs immediately following the sign COURSE* serves to assure consumers that, indeed, the singular, and not the plural, is the appropriate interpretation of the sL message.

It could well be argued that this miscue also provides evidence for a monitoring function of the whole process that enables correction of tL utterances by comparison of the intent and information value of the tL utterance with the intent of the sL message, which has been temporarily stored and, in part, retained for this purpose. That such a monitoring (or internal feedback) function exists, however, does not mean that it is constantly activated by interpreters nor that interpreters always act on the information provided by their own internal monitoring of their performance. That this seems to be the case is evident from the scarcity of miscue corrections found in the data.

Although in the example just presented the interpreter was able to recognize and correct the perception miscue, the usual result is that perception miscues are unrecognized and, hence, uncorrected by the interpreter. The interpreter, in fact, may be completely confident in interpreting the misperceived sL message and assume that the sL message has been accurately received. The significance of miscues caused by misperceptions is that, unlike other types of miscues, there is generally no possibility that consumers can   detect that a miscue has occurred; thus they cannot compensate for the miscue (Cokely, 1982); e.g.:

sL: "...*The matiere courses were taken in other departments*...."

```
                                        (brow raise        )
tL:  ". .SECOND-THING OTHER-inc NEXT   A-LIST-OF-THINGS
                    ___nod___
SHIFT-TO INDEX M-A-T-U-R-E   THAT-If hand
                              '5'_____
                                              _____th
INDEX-If hand             OTHER P-T-S
_____INDEX                          5:CL each to If ..."
```

Back translation of tL: "...second item oth- next list of items first one second one mature that there other p-t-s each-one careless p-t-s"

There are two factors that support the deduction that the interpreter's production of M-A-T-U-R-E represents a perception miscue. The first is that the speaker's pronunciation of the word *matiere* was such that it may have sounded to the interpreter as if the speaker actually said "mature." (Context, of course, should have provided the interpreter with sufficient information to determine that the speaker could not have intended "mature." Thus this example might also serve as evidence of a problem in the preliminary processing stage.) Second, this is the first of four instances of the lexical item matiere in the presentation; in subsequent occurrences (all outside the sample data) the interpreter produced more accurate tL renditions: M-A-T-I-E-R (twice) and M-A-T-I-E-R -E (once).

It seems undeniable, not only from the miscue evidence presented above but also assuming any logical ordering of the events/processes involved in interpretation, that sL information must be accurately perceived/received by the interpreter in order for accurate interpretation to occur. While perception/reception of the sL message does not guarantee accurate interpretation of that message, it is, nonetheless, a necessary condition for accurate interpretation to occur.

Preliminary processing

As noted above, the recognition of individual lexical items or set of lexical items that comprise the sL message often requires an understanding of prior semantic and syntactic context. Certainly this is the case in determining an appropriate meaning for a lexical item from the range of possible meanings that that lexical item might convey. Regardless of which theory (e.g., multiple levels of processing or the Word Initial Cohort) best explains how such processing occurs, there are miscue data that demonstrate the consequences of failing to make the appropriate lexical determinations at this stage of the process; e.g.:

sL: "....the next time we have a law we testify with one voice..."

(brow raise)—nod
tL: "...WE MUST PASS LAW   US-TWO If-FIT-IN-rt ONE VOICE..."

Back translation of tL: ". . .we must pass [a] law, yes the two of us
merge together [using? with?] a single vocal apparatus."

An additional piece of information helps to understand this example: at no time during this example, nor in the 10 seconds preceding and following, did the interpreter's lag time exceed 1 second. Thus, it is probably the case that the necessary condition— sufficient contextual information—for preliminary processing to occur did not and could not obtain in this situation.

It would seem that the interpreter has not realized that the sL *one voice* is used metaphorically; the interpreter has used the sign VOICE, which is not used metaphorically in ASL (for obvious reasons) and conveys only one of the meanings of the English word *voice*. Although this is the primary meaning of *"voice"* and may be meant most frequently when the word is used, it is evident from the context that it is not the meaning intended by the sL utterance.

It could be argued that the interpreter failed to process the sL phrase *testify with one voice;* but this is only partially borne out by the interpreter's performance. Although the sign If-FIT-IN-rt (which means 'synchronize', 'be in harmony with', 'complement') constitutes the initial portion of what could be an acceptable and accurate interpretation, the intrusion ONE VOICE not only results in an anomalous tL utterance but also represents, at best, a rendition of the sL message based on a shallow or superficial processing of the sL lexical items.

This example provides evidence for the need to process properly incoming sL lexical information, but it could also provide evidence for the need to maintain a sufficient time lag. It may very well be that the primary cause for this miscue is insufficient time lag (which is a function of short term message retention), and that failure to process the incoming sL information adequately is either a secondary cause or a necessary result of the primary cause.

It is, however, not always the case that insufficient time lag is the cause of miscues resulting from unprocessed or insufficiently processed sL information. There is strong miscue evidence that even with increased lag time sufficient processing fails to occur. In the following example, the onset lag time is approximately 2.5 seconds.

    sL: *"... you notice that the language is very informal..."*

       (eye gaze at screen overhead)   (brow raise   )
    tL: "...   NOTICE LANGUAGE

                  mm   (brow raise)   nod
    "WELL" CONVERSE ALIKE DAILY I-N-F-O-R-M-A-L...

    Back translation of tL: '...Notice [the] language [is], well, talk casually like everyday informal..."

The preceding context, and the behavior of the speaker, make it clear that the sL lexical item *language* is being used to refer to a list of English words that appear on a checklist projected onto a screen. The message being conveyed is that the terms chosen for use on this checklist are such that they could be readily understood; i.e. the attempt was to avoid using jargon and, instead, to use terms that are "informal" and presumably, more readily intelligible to those using the checklist. The interpreter has had the opportunity to gain the contextual information necessary to understand this sL utterance. Preceding sL utterances were reasonably well interpreted, and the interpreter looked at the checklist being projected before producing the tL utterance. Thus, the interpreter had access to sL content and visual clues necessary to provide the basis for appropriate understanding of the sL message. Despite this, it is apparent that the appropriate meaning of the sL lexical item *language* was not identified nor selected by the interpreter. In this context the appropriate meaning is not conveyed by the sign LANGUAGE (which means 'sentences', 'connected discourse') but would be conveyed by the sign WORD (which means 'vocabulary', 'individual lexical items.').

It is conceivable that failure to process appropriately incoming sL information might result from interpreter fatigue. However, the miscue presented above occurs during the tenth minute of the interpreter's assignment, presumably when the interpreter has had time enough be accustomed to the speaker but not yet become fatigued. It should also be noted that miscues resulting from insufficient processing occur throughout the data sample without noticeable differences in whether they occur early or late in an interpreter's assignment.

It is clear that tL miscues result from failure to process sufficiently incoming sL lexical information—because of insufficient time lag, fatigue, or other factors. It is apparent that a necessary but not sufficient condition for processing to occur is that the interpreter gain adequate sL contextual information. This necessarily means that decreased time lag will preclude sufficient processing of incoming sL information. It also seems evident that much of this processing must occur prior to short term message retention or, more likely, as a result of continuing adjustments to information already retained in short term storage. In either event, it is clear that there is a time lag threshold below which sufficient contextual information cannot be obtained; without it accurate and thorough processing is impossible.

Short term message retention

Because the nature of simultaneous interpretation means that the interpreter is presented with gradually unfolding, multi-leveled, incoming linguistic messages, it is apparent that the interpreter must conserve information over a span of time in order to gather sufficient contextual input needed to comprehend the linguistic messages. A direct indication of the importance of and necessity for short term memory in the interpretation process can be gained by examining interpreter lag time. As noted in Chapter 5, there is evidence of a definite relationship between lag time and miscue occurrence: with increased lag time fewer miscues are produced, and conversely, with decreased lag time more miscues are produced.

However, it would appear that there are several levels or perhaps types of memory that may need to be exercised before an accurate interpretation can be produced. Certainly one level or type of memory is sentential short term memory. This is the intra-sentential memory that is required to understand the meaning of lexical items within a given sentence. Onset lag time provides a direct indication of the intra-sentence information that an interpreter gains before producing an interpretation; it also indicates the extent to which short term memory is being exercised. Failure to gain sufficient intra-sentential information may result in inappropriately processed lexical items as seen above under preliminary processing (cf. 4.0), or it may interfere with message reception—recognizing and rectifying possible misperceptions (cf. 3.0).

The interpreter needs short term memory to gain intra-sentential information, but interpreters may overextend the limits of their short term memory; i.e. if interpreters wait to produce an interpretation for a length of time that exceeds the limits of their short term memory, then information will be lost. It is not within the scope of this study to provide an in-depth discussion of short-term memory. However, the loss of information is accounted for by all models and theories of short term memory. For example, those theories that suggest a "stacking" of items in short term memory generally hold that the first unit in a sequence of units is likely to be lost when the number of units to be retained exceeds one's "stacking" capacity. In any event, it is evident that well-developed short term message retention is an essential stage in the interpretation process, not only because failure to use short term retention by waiting for sL information can result in the kinds of miscues examined above, but also because information loss occurs when interpreters are forced to, or attempt to, retain more information than their short term memories are capable of retaining; e.g.:

sL: *"...Once we had the first doctored generation then I think we did something that to me is very important..."*

```
    (brow raise            (head, eyes to rt
tL: ...FINISH     (1h)HAVE    CHANGE     FINISH
           ))    _t_                        rhet-q
MATCH-TO-rt GEAR,   ME   FEEL TRUE IMPORTANT   WHY...
```

Back translation of tL: '...after possess change completed integrated, Me? I felt really important. Why?...

The average onset time lag for this interpreter is 1.7 seconds with a range of 1-4 seconds. In this example, the onset lag time is 4 seconds. Thus the interpreter is operating at the upper (personal) limit of time lag. It also seems that for this interpreter, at least, content integrity is not maintained when operating at the upper time lag limit. In this instance the loss of sL information (*...then I think we did something that...*) in the tL interpretation results in a tL message that is quite different from the sL message.

With an onset lag time of 4 seconds and given the speaker rate at this point, the interpreter starts the production of the tL message at the same time that the speaker begins to produce that portion of the sL message that the interpreter ultimately omits. Since the lag time in this example (4 sec.) represents the lag time ceiling exhibited by this interpreter, it is conceivable that the sL information conveyed during that time (4 sec.) maximally occupied the interpreter's short term memory. If, for this interpreter, words are considered individual units in short term memory (as seems likely given an overall average lag time of 1.7 sec.), then the oft-quoted "7±2" unit storage capacity for short term memory (Miller, 1956) would seem to obtain, since tL production commenced after 7 sL words had been uttered. Consequently, at that point, short term retention of new sL information cannot occur until short term memory is no longer maximally occupied.

While the general expectation in simultaneous interpretation would seem to be that in short term memory there is an on-going "replacement" of old units with new units, thus maintaining an information-flow equilibrium, this does not seem to be the case in this example. Rather, it appears that no new sL information was retained in short term memory until all or most of the old information had been expressed in a tL utterance. That this, indeed, seems to be the case is evidenced by the fact that the information omitted ("...*then I think that we did something that*...") consists of the same number of units (again assuming that the interpreter is processing words as individual units) as the initial portion of the sL message. Another indication that information-flow equilibrium was not maintained is the fact that, while the onset lag time in this example was 4 sec., the lag time immediately following the omitted portion is 1 sec. Thus, the interpreter has "caught up" with the speaker by ignoring a portion of sL information equal to that portion of information retained in short term memory.

An interesting question and a fruitful area of research raised by this study is the "chunking" of information units by interpreters and the short term retention of those "chunks." The data in this study clearly represent a range of information-chunking abilities from Int. 3 who, with an average lag time of 1.7 sec., apparently treats individual lexical items as "chunks," to Int. 6 with an average lag time of 4.8 sec., who apparently "chunks" information quite differently. Systematic investigation of lag time and information "chunking" would undoubtedly reveal a variety of "chunking" strategies that may be useful in education programs for students of interpretation and aspiring interpreters.

It is undeniable that a major stage in the interpretation process is short term message retention. It is also clear that an information-flow equilibrium must be maintained by the interpreter in order that sL information not be omitted from the tL message. What is crucial about the short term message retention stage is that failure to gain sufficient intra-sentential contextual information (which is directly related to lag time which, in turn, is an overt manifestation of short term message retention) skews or limits accurate comprehension of the sL information. Short term retention of sL information, then, is a necessary but not sufficient requirement for accurate comprehension of the sL message which, in turn, is a necessary but not sufficient condition for accurate interpretation to occur.

Semantic intent realized

For this and subsequent medial stages of the interpretation process, it becomes increasingly more difficult to identify miscues that are clearly and singularly caused by a problem at these stages. It is just as plausible to argue that a miscue apparently resulting from medial stage processing difficulties may be the result of prior processing difficulties. The stages of the process are, as it were, nested. Thus, miscues may be traceable to temporally and logically initial and final stages, but tracing miscue causes to medial stages is not so readily done. From an information processing perspective, since the output of a given stage in the process constitutes the input for the next stage in the sequence, a miscue apparently arising in a later stage may be due to faulty input from a former stage.

Assuming that preceding stages of the process have been accurately and sufficiently carried out, the interpreter reaches a point where the sL message or a portion of that message is understood. It is probably more accurate to say that the interpreter reaches a point where some level of meaning or semantic intent must be ascribed to the sL information. Whether the meaning or semantic intent ascribed by the interpreter is in harmony with or identical to the speaker's meaning or semantic intent will be determined by the contextual information the interpreter has available and by the interpreter's accurate understanding of cohesive and referential relationships in the sL message.

As mentioned above, prior stage processing difficulties or distortions will lead the interpreter to ascribe a meaning or semantic intent to the sL message that is at odds with the meaning or semantic intent of the speaker. Thus, in the following example the tL message clearly conveys a meaning and semantic intent quite different than those intended:

sL: *"What do I mean by these policy decisions?"*

nod	brow squint	tl
tL: " POLICY	MEAN #WHAT	"WELL" ..."

Back translation of tL: 'Policy means what? Well...'

In this example the tL message conveys a meaning different from that of the sL. With the onset lag time here of 4 sec., one could argue that insufficient short term message retention has caused this miscue. Thus, although the tL semantic intent is different from the sL intent, there is at least one plausible prior processing explanation for this miscue. There are, however, other miscues in which the sL semantic intent differs from the sL semantic intent and for which prior processing difficulties or distortions are a less likely explanation; e.g.:

sL: *"...then we established the mode in which we were going to test..."*
    <u>   cond</u>
tL: ...AND FINISH, ME ESTABLISH HOW #WILL

        <u>   nod</u>
TEST M-O-D-E(hd) ————

Back translation of tL: "...and when finished, I set-up how I would test the mode, yes..."

In this instance the tL meaning clearly differs from that of the sL. With an onset lag time of 1 sec., it would seem unlikely that short term message retention difficulties *per se* were the cause of this miscue. In fact, the tL production of M-O-D-E was initiated 2.5 sec. after the sL production of *mode*, which is only slightly greater than the interpreter's average lag time of 1.7 sec. It might alternately be argued that preliminary processing difficulties caused this miscue. However, the fact that the interpreter maintained a minimally adequate medial lag time would indicate that sufficient contextual information was available to ascribe a more appropriate meaning than that of the tL utterance.

One indication that the cause of this miscue is the interpreter's misunderstanding the sL message (and hence ascribes a different or distorted meaning to it) is the ordering of information and the syntactic and semantic relationships of the lexical items in the sL and tL messages. According to the sL message, what was determined was how the test would be administered (i.e. the mode or protocol), but according to the tL message what was determined was how the test protocol would be tested. The fact that the tL message indicates that the interpreter has rearranged and altered the relationship of sL information units would seem to indicate that the rearrangement occurs at a post-preliminary processing stage and at a post-short term message retention stage (unless, of course, one adheres to an interpretation process model that places the entire burden of comprehension on early processing stages).

It is evident that at some point the interpreter must attribute some meaning to the sL message and then proceed to express that meaning in the tL. Although clearly there is some level of meaning attributed during the preliminary processing stage, it seems intuitively and linguistically accurate to posit a reconstruction stage during which the information values of sL lexical items ascribed during preliminary processing are adjusted as more of the sL message unfolds. It is when adjustments are not made or when inappropriate adjustments are made that the sL meaning and semantic intent is not accurately understood or realized by the interpreter. The monitored reconstruction of sL information is also essential if the interpreter is to avoid ascribing meaning or semantic intent that has no apparent basis in the sL text or context; e.g.:

> **sL:** "...*we* [Sign Language interpreters and spoken languag interpreters] *testify with one voice and not jeopardize standards* [c interpretation that we wish the law to specify]..."

>   (brow raise
> **tL:** ...US-TWO If-FIT-IN-rt ONE VOICE AND NOT MAYBE HAPPEN

>   )   <u>nod</u>   <u>nodding</u>
> DESTROY   US-TWO WORK TOGETHER ———

> **Back translation of tL:** '...[the] two of us merge one voice and not possibly result in [the] destruction yes of us two working together yes...'

In this example, there is no clear reason why the interpreter has understood the sL *jeopardize standards* to mean "the possibility of destroying the working relationship of Sign Language and

spoken language interpreters." Were this the result of a distortion
in the preliminary processing stage, one would expect it to result
in either a lexical glossing intrusion (as is the case with *voice* and
V̲OICE) or, as in the previous example by the same interpreter, the
use of fingerspelling (e.g. sL *mode* and tL M-O-D-E). There is no
textual or contextual reference or allusion to a weakening
relationship between the two groups, which might help to explain
this misunderstanding. Also, since the onset lag time was 1 sec.
and since there were 8 sec. of speaker silence immediately
following the sL word *standards,* it cannot be that the interpreter
was influenced by the ensuing sL utterance.

Clearly this example provides a case in which the meaning and
semantic intent of the speaker was not understood by the interpreter. The misunderstanding is of such a nature that it cannot be
satisfactorily accounted for by claiming distortion or breakdown
of the short term message retention stage nor of the stages
preceding that stage. Given the educational background of this
interpreter (B.A.+), it would seem inconceivable that this
interpreter would not understand the meaning of *jeopardize
standards.* However, it is obvious from the tL utterance that the
meaning and semantic intent realized by the interpreter is not at
all in harmony with the popularly understood meaning nor the
meaning intended by the speaker.

It is likely that this example represents a case of faulty
prediction or expectation on the interpreter's part. That is, given
the time lag of 1 sec. in this example, the interpreter obtains only a
limited amount of sL information before producing a tL
interpretation. With limited sL input, the interpreter anticipates
(in this case erroneously) the next lexical items that the speaker
will utter. The interpreter heard "and not jeopardize" and then
acted on what was expected to follow it: "our working
relationship." The prediction was erroneous; the speaker actually
said "standards" (this is also an instance of what might be termed
a type of "speaker miscue" since the collocation "jeopardize

standards" might be considered unconventional or unusual). That the interpreter's miscue is, in part, due to faulty prediction is certainly consistent with the notion that comprehension of texts is based on frames (Tannen, 1979) and addressee expectations. Certainly the more usual way of expressing the speaker's intent in this case would be "and not compromise standards." Had the interpreter's lag time been greater, it is unlikely that this misprediction would have occurred, because the interpreter would have been able to realize that the intent of the speaker's message was not "jeopardize our working relationship" but rather "compromise standards."

Since subsequent stages of the interpretation process are predicated upon whatever meaning and semantic intent the interpreter ascribes to the sL message, it is clear that the interpreter must accurately understand the sL message in order to render an accurate interpretation. It may well be that the semantic intent realization stage is simply the point at which the results or output of previous stages are integrated into a meaningful whole. Thus, the reconstituted meaning will be positively or negatively affected by the integrity and accuracy with which preceding process stages have been executed. Nonetheless, the fact remains that what is not understood cannot be interpreted and what is incorrectly understood will be incorrectly interpreted. As with all stages of the interpretation process, comprehension of the sL message is a necessary, but not sufficient, condition for accurate interpretation to occur.

Semantic equivalence determined

Once the interpreter has ascribed some meaning or semantic intent to the sL message, it is essential that that ascribed meaning or intent be considered in light of the target language and the target culture. It is at this point that the interpreter's focus and attention must be on the meaning and semantic intent of the sL message and not on the sL form. As Nida and Taber (1974: 105) point out "... it is the content which must be preserved at any cost; the form, except in special cases, such as poetry, is largely secondary, since within each language the rules for relating content to form are highly complex, arbitrary and variable...." Thus, if the interpreter has not extracted meaning from the sL message and is simply processing the form of the sL message, miscues will arise because of the fact that there is not a one-to-one relationship between sL forms and tL forms.

> **sL:** "...*the next time we have a law we testify with one voice*..."
> (brow raise)---nod
> **tL:** WE MUST PASS LAW   US-TWO If-FIT-IN-rt   ONE VOICE
>
> **Back translation of tL:** "...we must pass (a) law yes (the) two of us merge one voice..."

This example has been discussed above (p. 126) as an instance of insufficient preliminary processing. It also serves as an instance of interpreter failure to transfer the meaning of the sL message to the tL. The resultant transfer of sL form not meaning yields a tL utterance that tL users do not use or understand metaphorically. Not only has the interpreter simply transferred the sL form and failed to transfer the meaning of the sL utterance, but the interpreter, by simply transferring the sL form, has also failed to recognize (or if recognized, failed to act on that recognition) that the consumer group attaches certain (negative) cultural values and attitudes to the lexical item VOICE which are likely to add difficulties to consumers' efforts to recover the intended sL meaning. These values and attitudes center in the historic imposition of oral-aural means of communication upon Deaf people by hearing people and the concomitant suppression and rejection of ASL. That the speaker is a hearing person whose attitude towards Deaf people and towards ASL may not be fully

clear to Deaf consumers increases the probability that the tL
utterance will be taken negatively.

In the example above, it is conceivable that the interpreter did
not understand the meaning of the sL message and so chose to
transliterate the sL form. If this were the case, then this represents
a failure to realize the sL message intent and thus would provide
evidence for that stage of the process. There are, however,
instances in the data where it is clear that the interpreter has
accurately understood the sL message but has failed to determine
the semantic equivalence of that message; e.g.:

> **sL:**   "...*I just looked in frustration. It* (the instruction booklet) *meant
> nothing to me...*"
>
> (head recoil   ) (head, eyes down)   (hd eyes rt)
> **tL:**...BECOME-FRUSTRATED   "WELL"   <u>G</u>REEK TO ME ...
>
> **Back translation of tL:** .(I) became frustrated, well [it was] Greek to
> me..."

In this instance, it seems clear that the interpreter has
understood the meaning of *it meant nothing to me* but has chosen to
convey that meaning by using the sL expression "it was Greek to
me." This is quite different from the previous example, in which
the interpreter mirrored the form of the sL message. In this
example, the interpreter does adhere to sL form, but presents a
paraphrase in the sL of the intended meaning of the sL message.
(It could be argued that, at least connotatively, "it was Greek to
me" is not equivalent to *it meant nothing to me*. The former phrase
implies that the "it" was too complicated or complex for the
person uttering the phrase; however, the latter phrase carries no
such connotation.)

It is curious that the interpreter, having understood the sL
meaning, chose to present a sL paraphrase of that meaning rather

than one of several tL means of conveying that meaning. Thus, although the interpreter has understood the sL message and has executed accurately each stage of the interpretation process through the semantic realization stage, it is clear that the interpreter has failed to choose precisely the tL semantic equivalence of the sL meaning. Although the interpreter must understand the sL meaning before tL equivalence can be determined, understanding the sL meaning does not in itself guarantee that a tL equivalent of that meaning will be identified by the interpreter. In other words, determination of tL semantic equivalence must be a stage in the overall process distinct from determination of sL semantic intent.

Syntactic message formulation

Having determined the meaning of the sL message and its semantic equivalent in the tL, the interpreter must make certain syntactic and lexical decisions before conveying the tL message. The interpreter's ability to make these decisions accurately (i.e. to select appropriate syntactic structures and lexical items that will convey the semantic equivalent of the sL message) is predicated upon tL competence. It is at this point that the interpreter's focus must be on conveying a meaning (the semantic equivalent of the sL message) in the tL using tL syntactic structures and lexical items that are appropriate and acceptable in the tL. Ideally the tL syntactic structures and lexical items that are selected will not only convey the content of the sL message but will also, inasmuch as possible, reflect certain sociolinguistic aspects of the sL message (e.g. syntactic and/or lexical variation related to speaker's age or educational level). Failure to select and produce appropriate and acceptable tL syntactic structures and/or lexical items results in a tL utterance that, at best, conveys a meaning different than that intended by the sL and, at worst, a totally meaningless tL utterance; e.g.:

sL: "...[such a form would enable us to denote an objective score, noting instances of mistakes in grammar, mistakes in the use of vocabulary] *and mistakes in conservation if we were over-translating or under-translating or mistranslating...*"

<pre>
       (_____ nodding) t   _____ neg
tL: ...INDEX-middle finger AND MEANING , ---- rt-PASS-ON-TO-rt
_____th   _____cond   _____nod ____t.l
FOUL-UP , #IF TOO-MUCH , INTERPRET LESS NOT ENOUGH
                 _____t.l.
INTERPRET #OR OFF-THE-POINT ...
</pre>

Back translation of tL: '... third thing and meaning? [it is] not conveyed [it's] carelessly disrupted. If disrupted too much, then interpret less insufficient interpretation or digress..."

It is evident that the intended meaning is that an objective score could be determined if there were instances of over-translation, if there were instances of under-translation, or if there were mis-translations (any of which would result in a mistake of conservation of meaning). As put forth by the speaker, there are three conditions which result in mistakes in conservation of meaning —...*if we were over-translating, under-translating, or mistranslating.*

The syntactic formulation of the tL message is such that it is virtually impossible for consumers to recover the sL meaning. Apart from the fact that the tL message reverses the expected tL syntactic sequence of condition and result, the nonmanual signal used to indicate the condition is terminated prematurely by the interpreter. That is, if the nonmanual signal were maintained until the end of the tL utterance presented above, then consumers would have only to contend with the reversed sequence of result and condition in order to recover the sL meaning. However, as a result of the premature termination of the condition signal, the lexical items intended by the interpreter to convey the second sL condition INTERPRET LESS can only be understood as the result or consequence of the truncated condition.

This example provides evidence that the interpreter can execute syntactic signals that would be required to convey accurately the sL message: topic marking, negation, and conditional. Accepting for the moment that onset lag time here of 1 sec. precluded acceptable tL sequencing of condition and result, it is clear that more than competence in the tL is required in the accurate syntactic formulation of the tL message. There must be a monitoring mechanism, not unlike hypothesis testing, by which possible tL syntactic message formulations are checked for the extent to which they accurately and acceptably convey the semantic intent of the sL message. It is apparent in the example above that the syntactic message formulation was unmonitored. One could, of course, posit such a monitoring mechanism at each stage in the process by which the possible results of each stage are checked for the extent to which they accurately reflect the outcome of the preceding stage.

Unlike the preceding example, not all instances of inaccurate syntactic formulation of the tL message contain indications that the interpreter has the tL competence required to convey the sL meaning accurately. Many of these miscues are examples of sL message syntactic intrusion, in which the interpreter replaces sL lexical items with tL signs commonly glossed by those sL lexical items. Others are examples of sL syntactic intrusion, in which it is clear that the interpreter adheres to sL syntactic structures that do not appear in the sL message; e.g.:

sL: "...*thought that the one thing was to make a task analysis and make a listing of all the things that first needed to be done...*"

tL: ... ME FEEL ONE THING ME MUST ACT BEFORE ME TEACH

COURSE   ME MUST ANALYZE #WHAT INCLUDE IN*
                INDEX- cntr

THAT* INTERPRET (2h)INDEX-course...

Back translation of tL: '...I felt one thing I must do before I taught that course. I must analyze what [to] include in that interpreting course...'

What is significant about this tL utterance is not so much that it generally mirrors the syntax of the sL but that it intrudes sL syntactic structures and sL lexical items that do not appear in the sL message. Additionally there are none of the nonmanual behaviors that occasionally co-occur with sL transliterations (e.g. nod, tight lips, brow raise) even in those instances of stressed lexical items (indicated by an asterisk). It is apparent from the interpreter's performance that significant portions of the sL message were understood and yet were not conveyed appropriately in the tL. In fact, were this token the only basis for judging this interpreter's tL competence, one would be unable to make a case that the interpreter possessed sufficient tL competence to function as an interpreter in this situation.

The examples presented above make it clear that competence in the tL is a necessary prerequisite for interpretation to occur. However, as shown in the first example, competence in the tL by itself is insufficient for accurate interpretation. Acceptable tL syntactic structures and lexical items that accurately convey the sL meaning must be identified and selected. The degree to which an interpreter is able to do this is predicated on accurately under-standing the sL message and on the interpreter's competence in the tL. It is likely that an interpreter with more complete tL competence (if competence is viewed as relative and variable) may identify a greater number of possible tL syntactic and lexical strategies for conveying a given sL meaning. Such an interpreter may be in a position to select particular syntactic and lexical strategies according to different criteria than is an interpreter who is less competent in the tL. For example, while both interpreters might produce appropriate and acceptable tL utterances (and certainly this is a minimum expectation for accurate interpretation), the interpreter who is more competent in the tL may be better able to identify and convey tL equivalents for certain sociolinguistic aspects of the sL message. In other words, an interpreter who is more competent in the tL may be better able to render a more "complete" interpretation.

In any event, it seems clear that, regardless of the degree of competence in the tL, there must be a monitoring mechanism—or from an information processing perspective, a feedback loop—by which the interpreter is able to determine the "goodness of fit" between the sL semantic intent and the tL syntactic structures and lexical items selected to convey that semantic intent. This monitoring mechanism may actually be a sort of mental preview of tL message production, in which the interpreter, now in the role of cognitive consumer, "receives" the proposed tL message, analyzes that message and, if the proposed tL message meaning matches the original sL meaning, then the interpreter actually produces the tL message. If the meanings fail to match then the interpreter may select an alternate tL formulation of the sL meaning.

tL message production

Assuming that the interpreter has accurately formulated an appropriate tL message, the next stage in the process is to produce that message. Although syntactic and lexical miscues have largely been accounted for as inappropriate tL message formulations, there is one type of miscue that is qualitatively different. Since even native users of a language occasionally produce utterances that contain, for example, misarticulations, skewed intonation patterns, or spoonerisms, it would be unrealistic to expect an absence of these or similar behaviors in the tL message productions of interpreters. Although there are occasions in which it might be necessary for the interpreter to attempt consciously and deliberately to exhibit such behaviors (in order, for example, to interpret a recurring sL phrase that may intentionally contain one or more of these behaviors), the general expectation seems to be that the tL message will contain no greater occurrence of such behaviors than if that tL message were produced by a tL user who is not interpreting. While this may be an unrealistic expectation given the additional cognitive demands of the interpretation process, it is clear that interpreters do exhibit such production/articulation miscues. It is also clear that at least some of these miscues make consumer recovery of the intended sL meaning difficult if not impossible; e.g.:

sL: "*...and then we arrived at a consensus...*"

    <u>(brow raise)   t</u>   (eyes, head to rt   )
tL: ...AND   ME , DON'T-MIND   If-SAME-AS-rt   THINK...

Back translation of tL: '...and me? I don't care [one thing] is the same as [the other] I think...'

In this example, the interpreter has apparently decided to interpret the meaning of *concensus* with the signs AGREE If-SAME-AS-rt, which, in certain instances, would be an accurate and acceptable interpretation. However, the interpreter has misarticulated the sign AGREE, which requires the forehead or orientation toward the forehead as its initial locus of articulation. This misarticulation results in production of the sign DON'T-MIND, which requires the nose or orientation toward the nose as its initial locus of articulation. That this initial location displacement results in production of a sign that conveys a meaning that is at odds with the meaning of the sL message indicates that this displacement was not intentional on the part of the interpreter (assuming, of course, the felicity condition).

The point of this discussion is that even though an interpreter has accurately understood the sL meaning and has formulated an appropriate tL message to convey that meaning, there are miscues that arise during the last stage of the whole process, the production of that tL message. At the very least, these production miscues are similar in type and frequency of those miscues or misarticulations produced by native users of the tL in monolingual settings. It is possible, given the additional cognitive demands on the interpreter, that there are interpretation-specific types of misarticulations and that there is an increased frequency of occurrence of such misarticulations. In any event, it is clear that miscues occur during the tL message production stage that cannot be attributed to previous stages of the process.

Summary of Chapter 6

The purpose of this chapter has been to validate and illustrate with examples the major stages in the interpretation process model presented at the beginning of this chapter. While subprocesses and factors may influence the major stages of the model, verification and validation of those subprocesses and influencing factors through miscue analysis is beyond the scope of this present study. However, there is ample evidence and support for these subprocesses and influencing factors in the literature about perception, memory, information processing, and sociolinguistics.

Clearly, distortions or deviations occurring in or during a given stage of the process will affect subsequent stages in the process. This is because the stages in the process are interdependent and because miscues arising at logically and temporally prior stages form the information basis on which later stages are executed. It is, however, possible that the interpreter can recover from or repair prior stage miscues, especially if a monitoring mechanism exists and is activated at each stage. The interpreter's ability to access or activate such a monitoring mechanism may be constrained by the conditions of simultaneous interpretation: the interpreter may be processing more than one sL message at any given point in time. Thus, to present an admittedly simplified view of the processing of multiple sL messages: while sL message A is being produced by the interpreter (tL message production), the interpreter may be determining the tL semantic equivalent of sL message B, and may be receiving and preliminarily processing sL message C. One result of processing multiple sL messages simultaneously may be that the interpreter is less able to devote sufficient cognitive attention to monitoring the output of each or any stage in the process. Thus, miscues arising in prior stages are less likely to be recognized or repaired in subsequent stages.

On the basis of the discussion of each stage in the interpretation process, it is possible to make certain general statements about prerequisites for accurate interpretation. The order of these statements is related to the sequence of stages in the process and is not intended to indicate relative importance.

- sL messages must be accurately received by the interpreter.
- Repair of misperceptions is possible only to the extent that contextual information enables the interpreter to recognize that a misperception has occurred.
- Sufficient contextual information is necessary for the interpreter to determine the specific meaning of sL lexical items from the range of meanings those lexical items may convey.

- There is a lag time threshold below which sufficient sL contextual information cannot be available to the interpreter.
- At least intra-sentential short term memory is required to accurately understand the meaning of lexical items within a sL message.
- Maximum contextual information can be gained if the interpreter's short term memory operates on information "chunks" that encompass more than a single lexical item.
- The interpreter's ability to understand syntactic structures and lexical items in the sL message is dependent upon the interpreter's competence in the sL.
- What is not understood cannot be interpreted.
- What is incorrectly understood will be incorrectly interpreted.
- The simple transfer of sL form, instead of sL meaning, into the tL will present linguistic and, possibly, cultural difficulties for consumers.
- The interpreter's ability to select appropriate syntactic structures and lexical items is dependent upon the interpreter's competence in the tL.
- Interpreter misarticulations will be at least of the types and frequency of misarticulations of native users of the tL.

It should be evident that the stages in the interpretation process discussed above are not language specific. That is, there is nothing in the discussion or description of any stage that is unique to the English-ASL situation (except, of course, the fact that the modalities of the two languages are different. However, that fact does not alter the major stages of the process. It does add an additional influencing factor for interpretation between a signed language and a spoken language.). Consequently, there is reason to believe that the process model presented above is valid for interpretation between spoken languages, and interpretation between signed languages, as well as between spoken and signed languages. Certainly the model presented above is consistent with previous psychological research on simultaneous interpretation (e.g. Gerver, 1976; Moser, 1978) and is consistent with sociolinguistic research on communicative interaction.

Finally, this discussion of the interpretation process has raised several issues that warrant further systematic investigation. It would be extremely important to determine how much contextual information and support an interpreter must have before accurately understanding the meaning of a sL utterance. Another crucial area concerns the interpreter's "chunking" of information and the semantic or syntactic strategies used by interpreters to retain intra-sentential information. The process model presented here provides the necessary framework within which these and other significant issues related to simultaneous interpretation can be systematically addressed.

CHAPTER SEVEN

IMPLICATIONS AND APPLICATIONS

This chapter points out implications the model and analysis of miscues in the stages of the model has for interpreters and their consumers and suggests how these might be applied in the preparation and assessment of interpreters (and those who would be interpreters). Before discussing the implications and applications, however, it may be useful, given the minority status of the Deaf Community and its language, to address certain anticipated reactions to this study which may be less than positive.

It would be unrealistic to expect that all who read this study or learn of it indirectly will react with appropriate scientific objectivity or judicious detachment. The issue of language and the Deaf Community, as is true of linguistic minorities in general, is an emotion-laden one. Discussions of any aspect of a minority language—in this case American Sign Language as the target language for interpretation—are usually sharply polarized. The usual detractors maintain that the minority language lacks the complexity, sophistication, and status of the majority language and thus is unfit for any purpose except the casual conversations of those who are unsophisticated and uneducated. Parenthetically, one often suspects that opposition to the minority language is motivated as much by fear as anything else—fear of losing self-perceived status, fear of being shown to be in error, and fear of needing to learn the minority language and being unable to do so. The supporters, for their part, find themselves arguing on the basis of the potential inherent in any language that complexity, sophistication, and status will increase in accordance with the domains in which the language is allowed to be used. Further, the supporters argue, it is unreasonable and unfair to compare a minority language with a language that has enjoyed majority status for centuries.

Those who are opposed to ASL and who claim it is an inferior language may feel that this study supports their position by arguing that interpreter miscues are inevitable because of limitations inherent in ASL. Such an argument, however, overlooks several factors that must be considered if the results of this study are to be properly understood. Among these are three salient factors.

First, simultaneous English-ASL interpretation at professional conferences seems to be a relatively recent phenomenon. Indeed, the first conference at which it is documented that interpretation, not transliteration, was the expectation was the Third National Symposium on Sign Language Research and Teaching (NSSLRT) which was held in 1980. While ASL had been used at previous conferences (e.g. the First NSSLRT in 1977 and the Second NSSLRT in 1978), interpretation was almost exclusively from ASL to English and generally was conducted consecutively, not simultaneously. In general, when English was the sL, transliteration, not interpretation, was done. Although simultaneous interpretation of spoken languages has a documented history of approximately 40 years, simultaneous English-ASL interpretation is a much more recent phenomenon. Thus, the performance of simultaneous English-to-ASL interpreters at professional conferences may, in part, be a reflection of the relative novelty of simultaneous English-to-ASL interpretation at professional conferences.

Second, the professional evaluation/certification procedures of the Registry of Interpreters for the Deaf from 1972 until 1979 penalized candidates who did not "keep up with the speaker." That is, candidates who attempted to maintain a lag time that would enable them to interpret, rather than transliterate, were generally given lower scores than those who did not. In short, even on those sections of the evaluation that were to be interpreted, candidates were dissuaded from employing the necessary time strategy that would enable them to interpret. In addition, prior to 1979, those passages that were to be interpreted during the evaluation were almost exclusively limited to kinds of text that reflected the prevailing bias against ASL (Cokely, 1980); no expository monologues were included. This negative biasing in the evaluation/certification procedures directly affected preparation programs: because "success" was ultimately determined by the number of graduates who passed the evaluation, Interpreter Preparation Programs often structured their curricula to reflect the expectations of the evaluation.

Third, as noted in Chapter 1, research on Sign Language interpretation is extremely limited, and descriptive research on interpreter performance is not only limited but quite recent. In fact, the first descriptive research on interpreter performance in this country appeared shortly before the data in this study were collected (Cokely, 1982). This means that information that conceivably would be helpful to interpreters in assessing their own interpretation competence and identifying their strengths and weaknesses, has only recently been available. In addition, this study is the very first to provide descriptive information on the interpretation of expository monologues.

While some may read this as an apology or rationalization for some of the findings of this study, they are intended as neither. They are intended merely to provide a framework within which this study must be viewed. These factors, of course, must be considered in addition to the rather paradoxical truth of any microanalytic, descriptive research: the more one wishes to understand something, the more closely one must examine it, yet the more closely one examines something, the greater the likelihood that differences and irregularities will be found. Thus, at least from this perspective, it is not surprising that interpreter miscues occur. However, what is crucial, at least for this study, is the taxonomy of miscue types and the identification of miscue causes. It is from these that one can draw certain implications for interpreters and consumers and can suggest certain applications for the preparation and assessment of interpreters and would-be interpreters

Implications for interpreters

Perhaps the most significant implication for interpreters is that miscues do occur and certain types of miscues may occur despite preparation and conscious effort on the part of the interpreter to avoid them. Specifically, it is probable that sL misperception miscues and tL production miscues will occur with at least the same frequency as they do for native users of the languages in non-interpreting situations. Since these types of miscues are often undetected by the interpreter (as are other types of miscues), it seems appropriate for the interpreter to arrange for some level of external monitoring. This external monitoring can only be provided by another interpreter, since competence in both sL and tL is required to detect interpreter miscues. (Of course interpreters can arrange for delayed self-monitoring by videotaping their performance during an assignment, but because miscues cannot be detected until later, this procedure would seem of limited value in identifying and rectifying specific miscues in practice.) Clearly the more serious the consequences of interpreter miscues are for the consumers (e.g. in medical or legal situations), the more essential it is to have such external monitoring. Ironically, it seems to be the case that such external monitoring is marginally available and, when available, generally only in situations where the consequences of miscues might be deemed less serious (e.g. conferences or all-day meetings with two or more interpreters present).

A second implication is that interpreters must have appropriate levels of competence in both languages. If one expects to interpret in other than conversational situations, it is not enough to be conversationally competent in the tL. Given that there are specific differences, at least in message form and interaction norms for different discourse genre and settings, then the interpreter must be aware of these differences in both languages in order to render an accurate and appropriate interpretation in these different situations.

A third implication for interpreters is that maximum temporal synchrony of sL and tL messages is not only undesirable but also directly causes inaccurate interpretation. That is, the closer in time the tL message is to the sL message it is supposed to convey, the less likely it is that the tL message will be accurate and the less likely it is that the tL message will be acceptable in the tL. This necessarily means that the interpreter must develop the ability to maintain enough lag time (and, of course, use that lag time to process sL messages and prepare tL messages) to make accuracy and appropriateness possible.

A fourth implication, also related to the issue of temporal synchrony, concerns what can be termed "economy of cognitive effort." Given the complexity of the interpretation process, the cognitive demands on the interpreter can be reduced by increasing the portion of time that the interpreter is engaged in only one of two activities (delivering the tL message or listening to the sL message) and decreasing the portion of time that both activities must be engaged in simultaneously. The interpreter's ability to do this is directly related to the interpreter's lag time.

A fifth implication concerns interpreter behavior during those instances when the sL message or portions of it are not understood. Given the importance of contextual information for comprehension, the appropriate response to comprehension difficulties is to wait and listen until adequate contextual information can be acquired to aid comprehension. This response may run counter to the automatic response of immediate shadowing of the sL message. Of course, the ability to wait without fear of omissions is directly related to short-term message retention and lag time, both of which must be sufficiently developed to allow the interpreter to wait.

A sixth implication concerns speaker rate. Historically, interpreters have responded to speakers who speak at a rapid rate by asking them to slow down. However, since speaking rate seems to be a function of one's personality and, thus, is not easily alterable (Goldman-Eisler, 1972), this would appear to be a rather fruitless and misplaced request. A more effective request might be to ask speakers to pause more frequently. Such a request might not only be more easily and consistently honored by speakers but also, when honored, would enable the interpreter to utilize those pauses to maximum advantage by decreasing overall temporal synchrony.

A seventh implication concerns awareness of what can be called "consumer cognitive effort." Given that there are tL consumers who are not fluent in the sL or for whom the sL may be a second language, accurate and acceptable interpretation in the tL is a necessity, not a luxury. Thus, those miscues that are syntactic or lexical sL intrusions (which necessarily require competence in the sL to be understood) cannot be considered minimally or marginally adequate renditions of the sL message. The expectation of tL consumers is that they will be free to focus on the content of the sL message because it will be presented in a form in which they are fluent and with which they are comfortable (the tL). If sL intrusion miscues occur, these necessarily force tL consumers to access the intended sL meaning via a form (transliteration of the sL message) in which they may lack the competence necessary for comprehension. In other words, transliterations (syntactic or lexical) require that tL consumers understand the sL form in order to understand the intended sL meaning. Apart from the fact that some tL consumers may simply be unable to comprehend transliterations, there are those tL consumers who may have the necessary competence in the sL but who are also unable to comprehend sL intrusions. This is due, in part, to the cognitive dissonance created by sporadic and unsignalled sL intrusions in the context of the tL. Finally, the possibility exists that the cognitive demands on tL consumers created by such intrusions are such that appropriate and acceptable tL utterances immediately following sL intrusions may not be attended to. While some interpreters may feel that transliteration is an appropriate strategy to use if one cannot interpret, an understanding of the "consumer cognitive effort" required to accurately comprehend sL intrusions would indicate that, except under special circumstances, that strategy merely places the burden of coping with sL message form on the tL consumers. In short, by transliterating, interpreters abdicate their primary responsibility.

Implications for sL and tL consumers

An obvious implication for sL consumers is that, given the complexity of the interpretation task and the possibility of interpreter miscues, the possibility exists that they may be misunderstood by tL consumers. Thus, it would seem appropriate for sL consumers to phrase salient and crucial portions of their discourse clearly and unambiguously. Indeed, it might be an appropriate strategy to paraphrase those portions, after stating them once. This is particularly true of those speakers who choose to read papers rather than speak from notes at conferences. Because syntactic structures and lexical items used in written discourse tend to be more convoluted than those used in spontaneously spoken/signed discourse, reading a written paper may significantly increase the possibility of interpreter miscues.

A second implication for sL consumers is the fact that speaker pauses can be used by interpreters to reduce the cognitive demands on them and, consequently, increase the possibility of more accurate and appropriate interpretation. Thus, a second strategy sL consumers could adopt, in the interest of being accurately understood by tL consumers, would be judicious and appropriate pauses. While this will aid the interpreter and, ultimately the tL consumers, it may also increase the overall comprehension of those individuals who do not rely on an interpreter and have direct access to the sL message. This is also true of speakers who choose to read papers at conferences, since different pausing behaviors can be noted in reading aloud and in spontaneous discourse.

A major implication for tL consumers is that some misunderstandings are attributable, not to their own cognitive or linguistic limitations, but to the skewed tL input they receive. In fact, tL consumers' ability to recover intended sL meaning from certain types of interpreter miscues is a testimony to their cognitive and linguistic capabilities. However, there remain some miscue types from which the intended sL meaning cannot be recovered. While realization of this fact may not increase tL consumer comprehension of interpreted sL messages, it may allow tL consumers to retain a certain level of self-esteem and confidence in their own cognitive and linguistic abilities. This may be especially important for Deaf consumers whose educational experiences have generally convinced them that any and all communicative or linguistic misunderstandings are attributable to them.

Applications for preparation & curriculum development

Undoubtedly the most significant aspect of this study for Interpreter Preparation Programs and for those charged with developing curricula for such programs is the verified process model itself. This model, by providing a rather clear indication of the linguistic and cognitive skills needed to interpret, allows one to determine the extent to which a given program or curriculum enables a student to develop and refine those skills. Consequently, by asking of each course or set of course objectives whether and how it relates to the process model, one is able to identify superfluous or inappropriate courses or course objectives. Conversely, by using the process model and asking whether each stage is sufficiently addressed in a given program or curriculum, one is able to identify gaps or inadequacies. In short, the process model provides a basic statement of what a graduate from an Interpreter Preparation Program should be able to do (recognizing, of course, that experience will enable further refinement of skills).

In addition to this level of application of the process model there are a number of implications and practical suggestions for Interpreter Preparation Programs that can be drawn from this study. The order in which these implications and suggestions are presented does not reflect their importance.

Further implications

It is evident, both from the qualitative analysis in this study and from the process model itself, that one must have competence in both the sL and tL before interpretation is possible. This means that competence in both languages should be a prerequisite entrance criterion for admission to an Interpreter Preparation Program. It should be rather self-evident that the skills and abilities required to interpret cannot be acquired or learned until a person is already competent in both languages. A person cannot and should not be expected to learn ASL, for example, and at the same time learn how to interpret. The former is, quite clearly, a prerequisite for the latter.

A second implication is that students of interpretation must have no physiological conditions that would preclude clear access to the sL in interpretation. This means, for example, that in an English-ASL situation, the interpreter must be able to accurately receive and understand spoken English. An interpreting trainee's hearing ability must, at least, fall within a range that allows full access to spoken English. Those whose hearing ability does not fall within that range or who have no hearing ability at all will obviously be unable to interpret in an English-ASL situation. (Hearing ability, however, is not a necessary prerequisite for English-ASL translation; many deaf persons can and do perform such translation competently. Hearing ability is also not a necessary prerequisite for interpretation between signed languages) Similarly, a trainee's visual ability must at least, fall within a range that allows full access to signed ASL. Those whose visual ability does not fall within that range or who have no visual ability at all will obviously be unable to interpret in an ASL-English situation   Therefore, instructors in and directors of Interpreter Preparation Programs should be quite frank in this regard with students who apply for admission. Additionally, it would seem prudent and judicious for practicing interpreters to periodically and regularly have their hearing and vision examined.

A third implication is that simply because a student is a native speaker of English, for example, does not mean that the student possesses the analytic knowledge of the English language that is required of an interpreter. Communicative competence in the sL and tL, while a prerequisite for interpretation, does not in itself ensure a conscious understanding or knowledge of the syntactic structures and cohesion-creating devices of those languages. Consequently, specifically designed courses in both the sL and tL (e.g. English for Interpreters, ASL for Interpreters) or the integration of the content of such courses into other courses should be required in any Interpreter Preparation Program.

Practical suggestions

Because managing lag time and short-term message retention are pivotal in accurate simultaneous interpretation, it is appropriate to provide a number of instructional activities that will enable students to develop those skills. While some of these activities will be discussed below, it seems reasonable at this point to ask whether, in the initial stages of an Interpreter Preparation Program, the expectation and focus of instruction should be simultaneous interpretation or consecutive interpretation. A rather convincing case can be made that the cognitive demands on the interpreter are less for consecutive than for simultaneous interpretation (e.g. Lambert, 1984; Gerver, 1971) precisely because interpretation is delayed and not rendered simultaneously. Given this, it would seem appropriate to allow students to develop their interpreting skills without the added pressure of having to rely on undeveloped or underdeveloped lag time and short-term memory retention. Since consecutive interpretation inherently allows access to greater sL contextual information, a preparation program that focussed initially on consecutive interpretation would allow students to develop their interpretation skills before being asked to use those skills in the more demanding process of simultaneous interpretation.

Because the essence of lag time and short-term message retention seems to be the interpreter's ability to "chunk" information, one activity that would seem to be especially helpful in this regard is "delayed shadowing." The traditional shadowing task involves repetition of a stimulus item as quickly as possible. By gradually increasing response time (at 1 second intervals, for example), an instructor can simulate at least one of the conditions of simultaneous interpretation—producing one utterance while hearing or seeing another. Note that for this kind of task the student is not expected to interpret the stimulus material but is expected to respond in the language of the stimulus material.

A caution, however: this task, while developing lag time, may impart the mistaken notion that short-term memory retention consists of remembering lexical items. Thus, a second activity that does not focus on lexical items, delayed paraphrasing, would seem appropriate. (Paraphrasing, in and of itself, is a useful activity since it focuses on meaning, not form.) In delayed paraphrasing the student would be expected to render an ongoing sL message into the sL, using different lexical items and syntactic structures, at increasing response times. Delayed paraphrasing might also be thought of as intralingual simultaneous interpretation.

Both these activities, delayed shadowing and delayed paraphrasing, can be adapted to develop some of the additional internal monitoring skills an interpreter must possess. For example, if the instructor introduces noise into the stimulus material or omits a lexical item from the material, the student is forced to rely on contextual information to assist in making an educated guess about the meaning of the missing or distorted item. This enables the student to develop cloze skills in a situation that simulates simultaneous interpretation.

One ultimate aim of any preparation program is that graduates are able to provide accurate and acceptable interpretations. An activity that enables instructor and student to determine the accuracy of an interpretation is the use of "back-translations." The student, presented with a sL message, interprets into the tL and that interpretation is recorded. The interpretation is then translated or interpreted back into the sL. The original sL message and the back-translation can then be compared and the equivalence of the original sL message and the back-translated sL message can be determined. If done accurately, this procedure enables instructor and student to identify student strengths and weaknesses, as well as to discover processing difficulties.

It was suggested above that specifically designed language courses for interpreters can be included in the curriculum. Such courses would resemble text- and discourse-analysis courses in which students learn to recognize and identify features and characteristics of a variety of discourse/text types in each language. These courses would attend particularly to formulaic expressions, cohesion-creating devices, and other defining characteristics of different discourse genres. Structured properly, such courses could provide students with an invaluable opportunity to explore comparisons and contrasts between the two languages. Of course, the texts to be worked with should be spoken and signed texts that reflect the range of situations and settings in which interpreters normally work.

Finally, since theoretical and analytic discussions are but a pale reflection of first-hand experience, Interpreter Preparation Programs should provide opportunities for students to interact in each language in a range of discourse settings in which they alternately assume the roles of Speaker and Addressee. It seems improbable that an individual who has never prepared and delivered an expository monologue in a given language, for example, can interpret an expository monologue into that language. While it is clearly not possible to provide such opportunities for the entire range of settings in which interpreters work, it is possible to select certain prototypical interactions which would enable students to begin to internalize the importance of, and recognize the differences in, those sociolinguistic factors that influence any given interaction.

Implications for evaluation and evaluators

Perhaps the most significant implication of this study for the evaluation of interpreters, whether within the context of a preparation program or for professional certification, is that close synchrony of tL and sL messages is not a criterion by which accurate interpretation can be judged, except negatively. That is, the relationship between lag time and miscues, as shown in this study, is such that the shorter the lag time (i.e. the more synchrony between sL and tL messages), the greater the number of miscues. This means that evaluators should be concerned with lag time only to the extent that a too brief lag time results in miscues and that a too long lag time results in omissions of intended meanings.

A second implication is that interpreting is supposed to produce appropriate and acceptable tL messages for those whose first or only language is the tL. A difficulty in evaluations occurs when the determination of tL acceptability is made by one who also has access to the sL message (e.g. is another interpreter). Since it is unclear to what extent such a person's judgments may be influenced by having access to the sL message, it would seem appropriate to ask ask tL consumers, who do not have access to the sL message, to make such judgments. Interpretation accuracy can, of course, only be determined by one who does have access to both sL and tL text. However, the issues of interpretation accuracy and tL acceptability should not be confused, nor should a single individual be expected to make both determinations.

A final implication of the model presented here is that the sL materials to be used in any evaluation should be as realistic as possible and should represent a range of interpreting situations. In addition, those being evaluated should be provided with detailed information on as many of the influencing factors as possible (cf. Chapter 2), since they have a direct bearing on the interpretation. This means that more background information on consumers, interaction purpose, and setting must be provided in programs. Without this information, one may be unsure, for example, or whether a given sL utterance is intended sarcastically or seriously.

Implications for linguistics

In addition to the implications of this examination of interpreter performance for interpreters, interpreter trainers, and consumers, there are also important implications for the field of linguistics. Perhaps the most important implication stems from the taxonomy of miscue types presented in this study. If comprehension of any discourse is essentially a process of interpretation, then the miscues made by interpreters may also reflect those types of miscues (i.e. misinterpretations) that we all make when listening to others. Since textual or behavioral evidence of these miscues is not always readily apparent in uninterpreted situations, it would seem that studies of interpreter performance would yield much about the universal nature of language processing and language comprehension.

More specifically, it would seem that studies of interpreter performance would yield generalizable insights about such linguistic issues as the comprehension of referential devices, the saliency of cohesion-creating devices, and inferencing. Indeed, the fact that an interpreter is expected to act on such linguistic information by providing unrehearsed tL equivalents provides immediate evidence of the extent to which such discourse features of the sL are understood. In those instances where they are clearly misunderstood, linguistic evidence is provided about the nature and extent of the misunderstanding that is unavailable in uninterpreted situations.

It has been suggested that schemas or frames form the foundation for all types of discourse (e.g. Tannen, 1979; Freedle,

1979; Linde, 1981). Given that frames aid or determine the understanding of explicit input, the development and determination of inferences, and the nature of predictions or expectations, studies of interpreter performance would provide concrete evidence to address, among others, the following questions: What schemas are activated when a passage is comprehended? How and when are inferences and expectations generated? How and when are erroneous inferences and expectations corrected? How does one deal with information that is inconsistent with or irrelevant to an underlying frame?

Studies of interpreter performance also have definite implications for the area of semantics. Interpreters are expected to determine the appropriate meaning of the sL message and then to convey that meaning in the tL. Since the lexicons of any sL and tL, like those of any two languages, do not exist in a one-to-one relationship with each other, it is obvious that the interpreter must, at some level, identify the appropriate set of semantic primes from the semantic field of lexical items used to convey the sL message. The extent to which this is accurately done by the interpreter and the relative weights given to semantic primes can be determined by an examination of the tL text. Identification and specification of the semantic primes and the semantic field(s) of lexical items could, in fact, be aided by investigations of interpreter performance. Minimally such studies would provide evidence for the identification of universal semantic primes and semantic fields.

The very nature of interpretation is such that one is provided with an unrehearsed, theoretically equivalent linguistic indication of the extent to which a text has been understood. Thus studies of interpretation provide a window to many of the otherwise unobservable facets of the processes of text/discourse comprehension. This, then, is perhaps the most important implication of this study for the field of linguistics: studies of such processes or related issues can benefit considerably by examining the accurate and inaccurate interpretations of interpreters working in a variety of discourse settings.

Implications for future research

The model of the interpretation process presented in this study offers a framework within which systematic investigation of interpretation can occur. Such research will undoubtedly result in refinement and modification of the process model. Among the issues to be addressed by such research are the following:

A. In light of the cognitive demands during simultaneous interpretation, is it indeed the case that more accurate and efficient interpretation occurs when the sL is the interpreter's second or weaker language?

B. Do similar miscues occur during consecutive interpretation and, if so, do they occur with the same levels of frequency as reported here?

C. What strategies or techniques do interpreters with longer lag time use to "chunk" information? How do they sustain these longer lag times?

D. What tL discourse features (e.g. ordering of information) cannot be accurately executed during simultaneous interpretation?

E. What sL discourse features, if any, cause particular difficulty for interpreters (e.g. passive voice in English)?

F. What effects do interpreter miscues have on overall consumer comprehension of different interpreted discourse types?

G. To what extent does the signing/pausing ratio of interpreters reflect the expected signing/pausing ratio of the tL?

While a number of other fruitful areas for research have been raised throughout this study, these seven seem to be most significant. Future descriptive and experimental research, by addressing these and other issues within the context of the process model, will systematically increase our understanding of the process of simultaneous interpretation and the factors that influence that process.

Summary, Chapter 7

In this chapter I have suggested certain implications and applications of this study for Interpreter Preparation Programs, interpreters, and consumers. The major implication is that the process model provides objective means to determine the appropriateness of instructional and evaluational activities as well as assist interpreters in identifying their own strengths and weaknesses. It must be remembered that the data on which this study is based involves the language of a linguistic minority that has been oppressed and often maligned by members of the majority community. Additionally, it must be remembered that simultaneous English-ASL interpretation at professional conferences is a relatively recent phenomenon. These two factors form the framework within which the interpreter performance data in this study must be viewed. Finally, the sociolinguistically sensitive interpretation process model provides the basis for further systematic research in the area of simultaneous interpretation. Such research, drawing on this model, can provide insight into some of the issues raised by this study or can be directed at refining and modifying certain aspects of the process model.

CHAPTER EIGHT

SUMMARY

Chapter 1 detailed the need for a sociolinguistically-sensitive model of the interpretation process. This need is evident not only for Sign Language interpretation, but also for the interpretation of spoken languages. A review of the limited research in this area revealed that existing models of the process are information processing models which do not adequately account for sociolinguistic factors. Further, a review of the literature in the specific area of translation proved of limited value.

There followed in Chapter 2 a discussion of components of any communication interaction that have direct bearing on the interaction (setting, purpose, and participants). Each of these components was discussed in some detail. Then followed a discussion of those factors that are specific to the communicative message (form/content, channel/language, interaction norms) in which it became clear that specification of these factors was contingent upon selection of a specific discourse genre. Since the specific genre chosen for this study was expository monologue, these factors were specified accordingly.

Chapter 3 presented a discussion of the data collection procedures used. Also presented were the sampling procedures and transcription procedures used. Certain demographic information on the interpreters selected for this study was also outlined. Finally, a sample transcription segment was provided and discussed in depth to provide the reader with some understanding of the analysis procedure used in subsequent chapters.

Chapter 4 focused on temporal aspects and characteristics of the SL and TL texts. It was found that in simultaneous interpretation not only is maximum temporal synchrony not possible, it is also not desirable. It was also found that the cognitive demands on the interpreter are constant and that, by using pauses appropriately, the interpreter can reduce the cognitive demands by reducing the portion of time that SL message comprehension and TL message production must occur simultaneously. Among the interesting questions raised in this chapter is the question of lag time and what short-term message retention strategies are used by interpreters with greater lag times.

Chapter 5 presented a taxonomy of interpreter miscue types. The general categories were omissions, additions, substitutions, intrusions, and anomalies. Each of these categories was further sub-divided. The occurrence of each type of miscue was presented for each interpreter. As expected, those interpreters with shorter lag times produced more miscues, thus providing evidence that, for interpreters, maximum synchrony precludes gaining the contextual information necessary to render an accurate interpretation. Finally, this chapter briefly examined the extent to which certain non-manual behaviors of interpreters reflected expected TL norms in TL expository monologues. Evidence was found to suggest that the interpreter's TL production may be more informal than formal.

Chapter 6 presented a hypothetical model of the interpretation process and verification of the seven major stages of that process by identifying miscues caused by distortions or breakdowns in that stage. It was noted that the process model is non-language specific. That is, the major stages of the model are valid for interpretation between any two languages. Finally, a list of prerequisites for accurate interpretation, in light of the process model, was presented.

Chapter 7 presented implications and applications of this study and the process model. The most significant application of the model is the ability to assess objectively the appropriateness of curricula for Interpreter Preparation Programs and to assist interpreters in identifying strengths and weaknesses they may have. A major implication for Deaf consumers is the realization that misunderstandings may not always be due to their cognitive and linguistic abilities, but may arise from interpreter miscues. This chapter also discussed certain implications for linguistics, the most significant being the fact that interpretation provides a means of gaining access to the process(es) involved in text/discourse comprehension. Finally, this chapter discussed certain implications for future research in the area of simultaneous interpretation and presented several fruitful areas of investigation.

The findings of this study are based on a single discourse genre—expository monologue. Although other discourse genres would clearly necessitate different realizations of some of the factors influencing the process, the cognitive process of interpretation and the major stages of that process will remain constant regardless of situation or discourse genre. It is hoped that this study and the model presented herein have added to our understanding of simultaneous interpretation and have provided a framework within which future systematic research can occur.

Transcription Symbols

Transcription system from Baker and Cokely (1980).
Used herein with permission.

Symbol	Example	Explanation
CAPITAL LETTERS	**KNOW**	An English word in capital letters repre-sents an ASL sign; this word is called a *gloss*.
-	**FROM-NOW-ON**	When more than one English word is needed to gloss an ASL sign, the English words are separated by a hyphen.
-	**P-A-T**	When an English word is fingerspelled, the letters in the word are separated by a hyphen.
∩	**TRUE∩WORK**	When two glosses are joined by this curved line, it indicates a *compound* sign.
∪	**NOT∪HERE**	When two glosses are joined by this curved line, it indicates a *contraction*.
#	**#WHAT**	When this symbol is written before a gloss, it indicates the sign is a fingerspelled loan sign.
+	**DIFFERENT + + +**	When a plus sign follows a gloss, this indicates the sign is repeated. The number of plus signs following the gloss indicates the number of repetitions—e.g. DIFFERENT + + + indicates the sign was made four times (three repetitions).
*	**BORED***	An asterisk after a gloss indicates the sign is stressed (emphasized).

179

Symbol	Example	Explanation
( )	(ME)	Parentheses around a gloss indicate that sign is optional in the sentence; one could sign that sentence without the sign written in parenthesis.
,	YESTERDAY, ME	A comma indicates a syntactic break, signaled by a body shift and/or a change in facial expression (and usually a pause).
" "	"WHAT"	Double quotes around a gloss indicate a *gesture*.
(2h)	(2h)WHAT'S-UP	This symbol for 'two hands' is written before a gloss and means the sign is made with both hands.
alt.	(2h)alt.GUESS	The symbol 'alt.' means that the hands move in an 'alternating' manner.
" "	"open window"	Double quotes around a word or words in lower case indicate a mimed action.
" "	BECOME-SICK"*regularly*" LOOK-AT "*each other*"	Double quotes around an italicized word or words in lower case (after a gloss) in LOOK-AT"each other" dictate a specific modulation of that sign. The word or words inside the parentheses is the name for that specific modulation.
" " + " "	CORRESPOND-WITH "*each other*" + "*regularly*"	When a plus sign joins two or more modulations, it means those modulations occur simultaneously with that sign.
-CL	3-CL	This symbol for *classifier* is written after the symbol for the handshape that is used in that classifier.
↑	B↑-CL	An arrow pointing downward indicates that the palm is facing downward.
↓	B↓-CL	An arrow pointing upward indicates that the palm is facing upward.

Symbol	Example	Explanation
→	3 →CL	An arrow pointing to the right indicates that the fingers are not facing upwards. This is used to distinguish two sets of classifiers: 3-CL and 3→CL; l-CL and l→CL.
:	L:CL	This symbol indicates that the handshape is 'bent'—as in a 'bent-L' handshape where the index finger is crooked, rather than straight.
' '	(2h)4CL'line of people' l-CL'person come to me'	Single quotes around a lower case word or words is used to help describe the meaning of a classifier in the context of a particular sentence.
outline	1outline-CL'circular table'	This symbol indicates that the handshape is used to 'outline' a particular shape.
t	(2h)Ct-CL'huge column'	This symbol indicates that both hands in the classifier move or act 'together' to describe the referent—i.e. both hands have equal value and there is no 'dominant' hand.
rt lf cntr	rt-ASK-TO-lf ASSEMBLE-TO-cntr	The symbol 'rt' stands for 'right'; 'lf' for 'left'; and 'cntr' for 'center'. When a sign is made in or toward a particular location in space, that place or direction is indicated after the gloss. When a symbol like 'rt' is written before a gloss, it indicates the location where the sign began. So rt-GO-TO-lf indicates that the sign moves from right to left. These symbols refer to the Signer's perspective—e.g. 'rt' means to the Signer's right. The symbol 'cntr' is only used when that space directly between the Signer and Addressee represents a particular referent (person, place, or thing). If none of these symbols appear, the sign is produced in neutral space.

Symbol	Example	Explanation
lower case words	*pat*-**ASK-TO**-*lee*	Italicized words that are connected (via hyphens) to the gloss for a verb can also indicate the location where the verb began or ended. For example, if 'Pat' has been given a spatial location on the right, and 'Lee' is on the left, then the sign *pat*-**ASK-TO**-*lee* will move from right to left. These specific words are not used until the things they represent have been given a spatial location. These specific words are used in place of directions like '*rt*' or '*lf*'.
___	___-**GO-TO**-___ ___-**ASK-TO**-___	A blank line before and after a verb indicates that the verb is *directional*. These lines are only used in the text when discussing a particular verb and are not used in example sentences. In sentences, the blank lines are replaced by words, as shown above.
arc	*me*-**CAMERA-RECORD**-*arc* *me*-**SHOW**-*arc-lf*	When a gloss is followed by the symbol '*arc*', it means the sign moves in a horizontal arc from one side of the signing space to the other side. If another symbol like '*lf*' follows the symbol '*arc*', it means the arc only includes that part of the signing space

Symbol	Example	Explanation
@	5:↓-CL@rt	This symbol indicates a particular type of movement that is often used when giving something a spatial location. It is characterized by a certain tenseness and a 'hold' at the end of the movement. In this example, the classifier for a large mass is given a spatial location to the Signer's right.
↔	COMMUTE-BETWEEN-*here & rt*↔ *INDEX-lf & rt*↔	This symbol indicates a back-and-forth movement of the sign between two spatial locations. In the second example, the index finger points back and forth between a location on the left and a location on the right.
CAPITAL LETTERS	RESTAURANT *INDEX-lf*	When a sign is made with the nondominant hand. it is written in italics. When an italicized gloss is written under another gloss, it means both hands make separate signs at the same time. In this example, the dominant hand makes the sign **RESTAURANT** while the nondominant hand points to the left.
⟶	5:↓-CL-rt⟶	An arrow proceeding from a gloss indicates the handshape of that sign is held in its location during the time period shown with the arrow. In this example, the dominant hand 'holds' the 5:↓ classifier in its location on the right while the non-dominant hand points down (on the left side) with the index finger.

In addition to the transcription symbols used above that represent manual signals, there are also a number of non-manual signals in ASL that serve a variety of grammatical functions. Non-manual signals are represented on a superscript line above manual signals. The duration of each signal is indicated by the length of the superscript line or by the amount of space within the parentheses. Abbreviations are used to indicate specific non-manual grammatical signals. These are as follows:

  t - topic marking; consists minimally of a brow raise and a head tilt.
  q - yes-no question; consists minimally of a brow raise (different than that for topic) and forward head tilt.
  wh-q - wh - question; consists minimally of a brow squint and a head tilt.
  rhet-q - rhetorical question; consists minimally of a brow raise (different than those above) and a head tilt.
  neg - negative; consists minimally of a brow squint and a slight head shake.
  cond. - conditional; consists minimally of a brow raise and a slight forward head tilt.

There are also certain non-manual behaviors that function as modifiers. The transcription conventions for these and their meanings are as follows:

  cs - "very close in time or space"
  th - "without paying attention; carelessly"
  mm - "normally; regular; as expected"
  puff. cheeks - "a lot; huge number of; large"
  pursed lips - "very small; thin; narrow; smooth; quickly; easily"
  intense - "of tremendous magnitude; to an unusually great degree"

REFERENCES

Agar, M. *Ripping and Running: a formal ethnography of urban heroin addicts.* New York: 1973.

Albrecht, J. *Linguistik und Ubersetzung.* Tubingen: 1973.

Amos, F. *Early Theories of Translation.* New York: Columbia University Press, 1920.

Baker, C. & D. Cokely. *American Sign Language: A Teacher's Resource Text on Grammar & Culture* [1991, Gallaudet Univ. Press]. Silver Spring, MD: T.J. Publishers [Gallaudet Univ. Press], 1980.

Barik, H. A study of simultaneous interpretation. Ph.D. diss., University of North Carolina, 1969.

Barik, H. Simultaneous Interpretation: Qualitative & Linguistic Data. University of North Carolina, L.L. Thurstone Psychometric Laboratory, 1972. Working Paper 121.

Barik, H. Simultaneous Interpretation: Temporal & Quantitative Data. UNC: Thurstone Psychometric Laboratory, 1973. Working Paper 103.

Bassnett-McGuire, S. *Translation Studies.* New York: Methuen, 1980.

Bathgate, R. An Operational Model of the Translation Process, *The Incorporated Linguist* 19 (Fall 1980): 113-14.

Bathgate, R. Studies of Translation Models 2, *The Incorporated Linguist* 20 (Winter 1981): 10-16.

Battison, R. *Lexical Borrowing in American Sign Language.* Silver Spring, MD: Linstok Press, 1978.

Bienvenu, M. J.. A road being built..., *The Reflector* (9, Spring 1984): 28-32.

Blom, J. & . J. Gumperz. Social meaning in linguistic structures: code switching in Norway. In *Directions in Sociolinguistics*, ed. Gumperz & Hymes. New York: Holt, Rinehart & Winston, 1972.

Boomer, D. & A. Dittmann. Hesitation pauses & juncture pauses in speech, *Language & Speech* 5 (1962): 215-220.

Bradley, H. Smugglers' argot in the southwest, *American Speech* 31 (1956): 96-101.

Brasel, B. The Effects of fatigue on the competence of interpreters for the deaf. In *Selected Readings in the Integration of Deaf Students at CSUN*, ed. H. Murphy. Northridge, CA: California State University, 1976.

Brislin, R.W. (ed.). *Translation: Applications a&nd Research*. New York: Gardner Press, 1976.

Broadbent, D. Stimulus set & response set: Two kinds of selective attention. In *Attention: Contemporary Theory & Analysis*, ed. Mostofsky. New York: Appleton-Century-Crofts, 1970.

Brown, P. & C. Fraser. Speech as a marker of situation. In *Social Markers in Speech*, ed. Scherer & Giles. 33-62. London: Cambridge University Press, 1979.

Buhler, H. Suprasentential semantics & translation, *Meta* 24 (Dec 1979): 451-458.

Caccamise, F. *RID 1978 Convention Proceedings*, edited by F. Caccamise, J. Stangarone & M. Caccamise, Registry of Interpreters for the Deaf, 1979.

Caccamise, F. & R. Blaisdell. Reception of sentences under oral-manual, interpreted & simultaneous test conditions, *American Annals of the Deaf* 122 (1977) 414-421.

Caccamise, F. et al. (eds.). *A Century of Deaf Awareness in A Decade of Interpreting Awareness*. Silver Spring, MD: Registry of Interpreters for the Deaf, 1980a.

Caccamise, F. et al. (eds.). *Introduction to Interpreting for Interpreters/Transliterators, Hearing-Impaired Consumers, Hearing Consumers*. Silver Spring, MD: Registry of Interpreters for the Deaf, 1980b.

Capaldo, S. An apology for consecutive interpretation, *Meta* 25 (June 1980): 244-248.

Catford, J. *A Linguistic Theory of Translation: An Essay in Applied Linguistics*. London: Oxford University Press, 1965.

Chafe, W. Discourse structure & human knowledge. In *Language Comprehension & the Acquisition of Knowledge*, ed. Freedle & Carroll. Washington, D.C.: Center for Applied Linguistics, 1972.

Chafe, W. *The Pear Stories: Cognitive, Cultural & Linguistic Aspects of Narrative Production*. Norwood, N.J.: Ablex, 1980.

Charles, R. Conference Interpreting, *The Incorporated Linguist* 7 (Oct 1968): 79-85.

Chernov, G.. Semantic aspects of psycholinguistic research in simultaneous interpretation, *Language & Speech* (1979) Part 3.

Cokely, D. *Pre-College Programs: Guidelines for Manual Communication*. Gallaudet College, Pre-College Programs, 1979.

Cokely, D. Sign language: Teaching, interpreting, & educational policy. In *Sign Language & the Deaf Community: Essays in Honor of William C. Stokoe*, ed. Baker & Battison. 137-158. Silver Spring, MD: The National Association of the Deaf, 1980.

Cokely, D. Demographic characteristics of interpreters, *The Reflector* 1 (Fall 1981): 21-28.

Cokely, D. Editor's comments, *The Reflector* 4 (Fall 1982): 3-5.

Cokely, D. The Interpreted medical Interview: It loses something in the translation, *The Reflector* 3 (Spring 1982): 5-11.

Cokely, D. Metanotative qualities: How accurately are they conveyed by interpreters?, *The Reflector* 5 (Winter 1983): 16-22.

Cokely, D. When is a pidgin not a pidgin? An alternate analysis of the ASL-English contact situation, *Sign Language Studies* 1983 (38 1983): 1-24.

Colonomos, B. Reflections of an interpreter trainer, *The Reflector* 2 (Winter 1982): 5-14.

Comrie, B. Linguistic politeness axes: speaker-addressee, speaker-referent, speaker-bystander, *Pragmatics Microfiche* 1.7 (1976): A3-B1.

Congrat-Butler, S. (ed.). *Translation & Translators: An International Directory & Guide*. New York: Bowker, 1979.

Coulthard, M. *An Introduction to Discourse Analysis*. London: Longmans, 1979.

Coulton, P. A Study of the Validity & Reliability of the Comprehensive Skills Certificate Evaluation for Sign Language Interpreters: A Report to the Profession, *RID Interpreting Journal* 1.2 (1982): 16-37.

Craig & Lockhart. Levels of processing: A framework for memory research, *Journal of Verbal Learning & Verbal Behavior* 11 (1972): 671-684.

Crystal, D. & D. Davy. *Investigating English Style*. London: 1969.

Dixon, R. *The Dyirbal language of North Queensland*. London: Cambridge Univ. Press, 1970.

Droste, F. *Vertalen met de computer. Magelijkheden en Moeilijkheden*. Groningen: Wolters-Noordhoff, 1969.

Ferguson, C. Absence of copula & the notion of simplicity: A study of normal speech, baby talk, foreign talk & pidgins. In *Pidginization & Creolization of Languages*, ed. Hymes. 141-150. London: Cambridge University Press, 1971a.

Ferguson, C. *Language Structure & Language Use*. Stanford, CA: Stanford Univ. Press, 1971b.

Ferguson, C. & C. DeBose. Simplified registers, broken language & pidginization. In *Pidgin & Creole Linguistics.*, ed. Valdman. 99-128. Bloomington, IN: Indiana University Press, 1977.

Fielding, G. & E. Coope. Medium of communication, orientation to interaction, & conversational style. In Social Psychology Section Conference of British Psychological Society in 1976.

Fillmore, E.. Santa Cruz Lectures on Deixis, *Indiana Linguistics Club Papers,* Bloomington, IN , 1975.

Ford, L. The interpreter as a communication specialist. In *Third International Symposium on Interpretation of Sign Languages*, Royal National Institute for the Deaf, 91-98, 1981.

Forster, L. Introduction. In *Aspects of Translation*, ed. Booth. 1-28. London: Secker & Warburg, 1958.

Freedle, R. (ed.). *New Directions in Discourse Processing.* Norwood, NJ: Ablex, 1979.

Gerver, D. The effects of source language presentation rate on the performance of simultaneous conference interpreters. In *Proceedings of the 2nd Louisville Conference on Rate and/or Frequency Controlled Speech*, ed. E. Foulke. 162-184. Louisville: University of Louisville, 1969.

Gerver, D. Simultaneous interpretation & human information processing. Unpublished Ph.D. thesis, Oxford University, 1971.

Gerver, D. Simultaneous listening & speaking & retention of prose, *Quarterly Journal of Experimental Psychology* 26 (1974): 337-342.

Gerver, D. Empirical Studies of Simultaneous Interpretation: A Review & a Model. In *Translation: Applications & Research.*, ed. Brislin. 165-207. New York: Gardner Press, 1976.

Gerver, D. & H. Sinaiko. *Language Interpretation & Communication.* New York: Plenum Press, 1978.

Goldman-Eisler, F. Segmentation of input in simultaneous interpretation, *Journal of Psycholinguistic Research* 1 (1972): 127-140.

Goodman, Y. & C. Burke. *Reading Miscue Inventory.* New York: Macmillan, 1971.

Green, G. *Semantics & Syntactic Regularity.* Bloomington, IN: Indiana University Press, 1974.

Gumperz, J. Sociocultural knowledge in conversational inference. In *28th Round Table on Languages & Linguistics* in Washington, D.C., Georgetown University Press 1977.

Gumperz, J. & D. Hymes. *Directions in Sociolinguistics: The Ethnography of Communication.* New York: Holt, Rinehart & Winston, 1972.

Halliday, M. Anti-languages, *American Anthropologist* 78 (1976): 570-584.

Halliday, M. & R. Hasan. *Cohesion in English.* London: Longman, 1976.

Hargreaves, W. & J. Starkweather. Collection of temporal data with the duration tabulator, *Journal of the Experimental Analysis of Behavior* 2 (1959): 179-183.

Helfrich, H. Age Markers in Speech. In *Social Markers in Speech*, ed. Scherer & Giles. 63-108. London: Cambridge University Press, 1979.

Hill, J. Consecutive interpreting in advanced language work, *Meta* 24 (Dec 1979): 442-450.

Holmes, J. Describing literary translations: Models & methods. In *Literature & Translation*, ed. Holmes et al. 69-82. Louvain: Acco, 1978.

House, J. A model for assessing translation quality, *Meta* 20 (June 1977): 103-109.

House, J. *A Model for Translation Quality Assessment*. Tubigen, Germany: Gunter Narr Verlag, 1981.

Hurwitz, T. Interpreter's effectiveness in reverse interpreting: Pidgin Sign English & American Sign Language. In *A Decade of Interpreting Awareness*, ed. Caccamise et al. Silver Spring, MD: Registry of Interpreters for the Deaf, 1980.

Hymes, D. Models of the interaction of language & social life. In *Directions in Sociolinguistics*, ed. Gumperz & Hymes. 35-71. New York: Holt, Rinehart & Winston, 1972.

Ingram, R. A communication model of the interpreting process, *Journal of Rehabilitation of the Deaf* 7 (Jan 1974): 3-9.

Jacobs, R. The efficiency of interpreted input for processing lecture information by deaf college students, *Journal of Rehabilitation of the Deaf* 11 (1977): 10-15.

Jager, G. *Translation und Translationslinguistik*. Halle: 1973.

Jakobson, R. On linguistic aspects of translation. In *On Translation*, ed. Brower. 232-239. New York: 1966.

Jefferson, G. Side sequences. In *Studies in Social Interaction*, ed. Snow. New York: 1972.

Keenan, E. & B. Schieffelin. Topic as a discourse notion: A study of topic in the conversations of children & adults. In *Subject & Topic*, ed. Li. New York: 1976.

Kopczynski, A. *Conference Interpreting: Some Linguistic & Communicative Problems*. Poznan: 1980.

Labov, W. *The Social Stratification of English in New York City*. Washington, D.C.: Center for Applied Linguistics, 1966.

Labov, W. *Sociolinguistic Patterns*. Philadelphia: 1972.

Lakoff, R. *Language & Woman's Place*. New York: Harper & Row, 1975.

Lakoff, R. Persuasive discourse & ordinary conversation, with examples from advertising. In *Georgetown University Round Table on Languages & Linguistics,* Washington, D.C., ed. Tannen, Georgetown University Press,, 25-42, 1981.

Lambert, S. An introduction to consecutive interpretation. In *New Dialogues in Interpreter Education*, ed. McIntire. 76-98. Silver Spring, MD: RID Publications, 1984.

Landsberg, M. Translation theory: An appraisal of some general problems, *Meta* 21 (Dec 1976): 235-251.

Laver, J. & P. Trudgill. Phonetic & linguistic markers in speech. In *Social Markers in Speech*, ed. Scherer & Giles. 1-32. London: Cambridge University Press, 1979.

Levy, J. Translation as a decision process. In *To Honor Roman Jakobson*, 1171-1182. 3. The Hague: Mouton, 1967.

Linde, C. The organization of discourse. In *Style & Variables in English*, ed. Shopen & Williams. 84-115. Cambridge, MA: Winthrop, 1981.

Linde, C. & W. Labov. Spatial networks as a site for the study of language, *Language* 51 (1975): 924-939.

Llewellyn-Jones, P. Simultaneous interpreting. In *Perspectives on British Sign Language*, ed. Woll et al. 89-104. London: Croom Helm, 1981.

Longacre, R. *The Grammar of Discourse*. New York: Plenum Press, 1983.

Massaro, D. *Experimental Psychology & Information Processing*. Chicago: Rand McNally, 1975a.

Massaro, D. Language & information processing. In *Understadning Language*, ed. Massaro. New York: Academic Press, 1975b.

Maurer, D. The argot of the dice gambler, *Annals of the American Dialect Society* 269 (1950):

McLendon, S. Meaning, rhetorical structure & discourse organization in myth. In Georgetown University Round Table on Languages & Linguistics in Washington, D.C., ed. Tannen, Georgetown University Press, 284-305, 1981.

Miller, G. The magical number seven plus or minus two: Some limits on our capacity for processing information, *Psychological Review* 63 (1956): 81-97.

Miller, G. & J. Beebe-Center. Some psychological methods for evaluating the quality of translations, *Mechanical Translation* 3 (1958): 73-80.

Moscovici, S. & M. Plon. Les situations colloques: observations théoriques et experimentale, *Bulletin de Psychologie* 19 (1966): 702-722.

Moser, B. Simultaneous interpretation: A hypothetical model & its practical application. In *Language Interpretation & Communication*, ed. Gerver & Sinaiko. 353-368. New York: Plenum Press, 1978.

Namy, C. Reflections on the training of dimultaneous iInterpreters: A metalinguistic approach. In *Language Interpretation & Communication*, ed. Gerver & Sinaiko. 25-34. New York: Plenum Press, 1978.

NES Study Committee. Report of the National Evaluation System Study Committee Meeting. Registry of Interpreters for the Deaf, 1983.

Neumann Solow, S. *Sign Language Interpreting: A Basic Resource book*. Silver Spring, MD: National Association of the Deaf, 1981.

Newell, W. A study of the ability of day-class deaf adolescents to comprehend factual information usingg four communication modalities, *American Annals of the Deaf* 123 (1978): 558-562.

Newmark, P. Some notes on translation & translators, *The Incorporated Linguist* 8 (Oct 1969): 79-85.

Newmark, P. Twenty-three restricted rules of translation, *The Incorporated Linguist* 12 (Jan 1973): 9-15.

Newmark, P. Further propositions on translation, Part 1, *The Incorporated Linguist* 13 (Apr 1974): 34-42.

Newmark, P. Further propositions on translation, Part 2, *The Incorporated Linguist* 13 (July 1974): 62-71.

Newmark, P. *Approaches to Translation*. Elmsford, NY: Pergamon Press, 1981.

Nida, E. *Towards a Science of Translating*. Leiden: E.J. Brill, 1964.

Nida, E. & C. Taber. *The Theory & Practice of Translation*. Leiden: E.J. Brill, 1974.

Nida, E. & C. Taber. *Componential Analysis of Meaning*. The Hague: Mouton, 1975.

Ogden, C.K. & I.A. Richards. *The Meaning of Meaning*. London: Kegan Paul, 1927.

Oléron, P. & H. Nanpon. Recherches sur la traduction simultanée, *Journal de Psychologie Normale et Pathologigue* 62 (1965): 73-94.

Ostwald, P. *Soundmaking: The Acoustic Communication of Emotion.* Springfield, IL: 1963.

Palmer, J. *The Interpreting Scene: Proceedings of the Second National RID Convention.* Northridge, CA, Joyce Publications, 1974.

Paneth, E. An Investigation into Conference Interpreting (with Special Reference to the Training of Interpreters). Unpublished M.A. thesis, University of London, 1957.

Paneth, E. The interpreter's task & training, *The Incorporated Linguist* 1 (Oct 1962): 102-109.

Per-Lee, M. *Interpreter Research: Target for the Eighties, Gallaudet College.* ed. National Academy of Deafness. Washington, DC: Gallaudet College, 1981.

Pergnier, M. Language meaning & message meaning: Towards a sociolinguistic approach to translation. In *Language Interpretation & Communication,* ed. Gerver & Sinaiko. 199-204. New York: Plenum Press, 1978.

Popovic, A. Translation as communication. In *Translation as Comparison,* ed. Popovic & Denes. 5-24. Nitra: 1977.

Prince, G. *Narratology: The Form & Function of Narrative.* The Hague: Mouton, 1982.

Pronovost, W. An experimental study of methods for determining natural & habitual pitch, *Speech Monographs* 9 (1942): 111-123.

Propp, V. *Morphology of the Folktale.* Austin: University of Texas Press, 1968.

Quigley, S., B. Brasel, & D. Montanelli, ed. *Interpreters for Deaf People: Selection, Evaluation & Classification.* Washington, D.C.: Department of HEW, Social Rehabilitative Services, 1973.

Quigley, S. & J. Youngs, ed. *Interpreting for Deaf People*. Washington, D.C: U.S. Department of Health, Education, & Welfare, 1965.

Ramsay, R. Personality & speech, *Journal of Personality & Social Psychology* 4 (1966): 116-118.

Richards, I. Toward a theory of translating, *American Anthropological Association, Studies in Chinese Thought* 55 (Memoir 75 1953): 247-262.

Robinson, D. 10 Noted doctors answer 10 tough questions, *The New York Review*, July 12, 1980 1980,

Rose, M., ed. *Translation Spectrum: Essays in Theory & Practice*. Albany, NY: State University of New York Press, 1981.

Sacks, H. An analysis of the course of a joke's telling in conversation. In *Explorations in the Ethnography of Speaking*, ed. Bauman & Sherzer. 337-353. Cambridge: Cambridge University Press, 1974.

Sacks, H., E. Schegloff, & G. Jefferson. A simplest systematics for the organization of turn-taking in conversation, *Language* 50 (1974): 696-735.

Savory, T. *The Art of Translation*. Boston: The Writer, 1968.

Schegloff, E. Sequencing in conversational openings. In *Directions in Sociolinguistics*, ed. Gumperz & Hymes. New York: Holt, Rinehart & Winston, 1972.

Schein, J. Personality characteristics associated with interpreter proficiency, *Journal of Rehabilitation of the Deaf* 7 (1974): 33-43.

Scherer, K. Personality markers in speech. In *Social Markers in Speech*, ed. Scherer & Giles. 147-209. London: Cambridge University Press, 1979.

Scherer, K & H. Giles, ed. *Social Markers in Speech*. London: Cambridge University Press, 1979.

Searle, J. *Speech Acts: an Essay in the Philosophy of Language.* Cambridge: Cambridge University Press, 1980.

Seleskovitch, D. *Language, langes et memoire.* Paris: Lettres Modèrnes, 1975.

Seleskovitch, D. *Interpreting for International Conferences.* Washington, D.C.: Pen & Booth, 1978.

Shopan, T. & J. Williams. *Style & Variables in English.* Cambridge, MA: Winthrop, 1981.

Shuy, R. Subjective judgments in sociolinguistic analysis. In *Linguistics & the Teaching of Standard English to Speakers of Other Languages or Dialects*, ed. Alatis. Washington, D.C.: Georgetown University Press, 1969.

Shuy, R. Problems of communication in the cross-cultural medical interview, *ITL: Review of Applied Linguistics* 35 (1977).

Shuy, R., J. Baratz, & W. Wolfram. Sociolinguistic factors in speech identification. Center for Applied Linguistics, 1969. NIMHR Project MH 15048-01.

Sinclair, J. & R. Coulthard. *Towards an Analysis of Discourse.* London: 1975.

Smith, P. Sex markers in speech. In *Social Markers in Speech*, ed. Scherer & Giles. 109-146. London: Cambridge University Press, 1979.

Snow, C. Mothers' speech to children learning language, *Child Development* 43 (1972): 549-565.

Snow, C. & C. Ferguson, ed. *Talking to Children: Language Input & Acquisition.* Cambridge: Cambridge University Press, 1977.

Soubbotnik, S. Interpretation in the United Nations & its specialized agencies, *The Incorporated Linguist* 4 (Apr 1965): 38-41.

Steiner, G. *After Babel: Aspects of Language & Translation*. London: Oxford University Press, 1975.

Taber, C. Sociolinguistic obstacles to communication through translations, *Meta* 25 (Dec 1980): 421-429.

Tannen, D. What's in a Frame? Surface evidence for underlying expectations. In *New Directions in Discourse Processing*, ed. Freedle. 137-182. Norwood, NJ: Ablex, 1979.

Tannen, D. *Conversational Style*. Norwood, NJ: Ablex, 1984.

Taylor, W. Cloze procedure: A new tool for measuring readability, *Journalism Quarterly* 30 (1953): 415-433.

Tosh, W. *Syntactic Translation*. The Hague: Mouton, 1965.

Treisman, A. Monitoring & storage of irrelevant messages in selective attention, *Journal of Verbal Learning & Verbal Behavior* 3 (1964): 449-459.

Treisman, A. The effects of redundancy & familiarity on translating & repeating back a foreign & a native language, *British Journal of Psychology* 56 (1965): 369-379.

Turner, G. *Stylistics*. Middlesex: Harmondsworth, 1973.

Tytler, A. *Essay on the Principles of Translation*. Amsterdam: John Benjamins, 1978.

Van den Broek, R. & A. Lefevre. *Vitnodiging tot de vertaal wetenschap*. Muiderberg: Coutinho, 1979.

Vinay, J. & J. Darbelnet. *Stylistique comparée du francais et de l'anglais: Méthode de traduction*. Paris: Didier, 1958.

Warden, J. Suggestions for a course in oral translation, *The Incorporated Linguist* 5 (July 1966): 70-76.

Watzlawick, P., J. Beavin, & D. Jackson. *Pragmatics of Human Communication.* New York: W.W. Norton, 1967.

Whitehouse, J. Translation, *The Incorporated Linguist* 12 (Apr 1973): 32-34.

Wilss, W. *Ubersetzungswissenschaft: Probleme und Methoden.* Stuttgart: Klett, 1977.

Wilss, W. *The Science of Translation: Problems & Methods.* Tübigen: Gunter Narr Verlag, 1982.

Witter-Merithew, A., L. Siple, B. Carlson, & R. Dirst. *A Resource Guide for Interpreter Training for the Deaf Programs.* Silver Spring, MD: Registry of Interpreters for the Deaf, 1980.

Wolfram, W. & R. Fasold. *The Study of Social Dialects in American English.* Englewood Cliffs, NJ: Prentice-Hall, 1974.

Woll, B., J. Kyle, & M. Deuchar, ed. *Perspectives on British Sign Language.* London: Croom Helm, 1981.

Yngve, V. A framework for syntactic translation, *Mechanical Translation* 4 (1957): 59-65.

Zilahy, S. Quality in translation. In *Quality in Translation,* ed. Cary & Jumpelt. 285-289. New York: Macmillan, 1963.